Praise reports for Celebrate /

1

Celebrate Anglicanism

The Faith That Anglicans
Have Always Believed, Taught, and Practiced

Becoming a Fisher of Men
Revised Edition

 Anglican House
Publishers

This book is published by **Anglican House Publishers**.
You may contact us at http://www.ahpub.org.

Text editing by Katy Laundrie
Cover design and layout by Margie Hunter

ISBN-13: 978-0-9860441-1-3

Printed by ASIA PRINGING CO., LTD, Seoul, Korea

To Carol, the love of my life

Without her assistance, patience, dedication, and help with editing, this work would not have been possible.

Table of Contents

About the Author

Bud Davis, PhD, is an Anglican layman and educator. Born in Detroit, Michigan, and raised in the small town of Belleville, he attended Trinity Episcopal Mission where he was confirmed at the age of 12. He earned a Bachelor of Science degree at Michigan's Ferris State University, majoring in mathematics and chemistry. He and his wife Carol, with their first child, Charlie, moved to Southern California in 1968 where Bud began his career in education. He taught high school math and science for five years before moving into administration. He rose through the ranks as Dean of Students, Assistant Principal, Principal, Assistant Superintendent and, finally, Superintendent of Schools.

During his tenure as an educator, Davis attended California State University, Fullerton, where he earned a Master of Science degree in Educational Administration. He continued his education at United States International University in San Diego, earning the degree of Doctor of Philosophy in Human Behavior.

Bud and Carol's family grew to three children—two sons, Charlie and Jeff, and daughter Kristen. He and Carol now have six wonderful grandchildren.

Bud Davis is currently an instructor at the University of California, Los Angeles (UCLA), where he teaches credential classes for Career and Technical Education teachers and serves as an academic coordinator for that division.

Dr. Davis is a member of the Executive Committee of the Diocese of Western Anglicans. He and his wife, Carol, are members of Saint James Anglican Church in Newport Beach, California, where he currently serves on the Vestry and the Finance Committee. He was chairperson of the St. James Rector Search Committee. Bud and Carol are active in prayer ministry and have been leaders in the Marriage Encounter, Anglican Faith Alive, Alpha, Life in the Spirit, and Cursillo programs.

Forward

Celebrate Anglicanism is an extremely accessible introduction to Anglicanism — and in particular to its North American expression. For any who want to understand the basics of Christian Faith and the way that Faith has come to be handed on by those who would describe themselves as Anglican Christians this book covers all the basics.

Celebrate Anglicanism is written by a layman for the laity of the Anglican Chruch. The book is for those who are curious, who want to learn, who need basic knowledge. It is for ordinary Christians and those who are considering claiming their vocations as laymen and women in the world. The book is an invitation to becoming a disciple, and being informed enough to invite others into following Christ as committed and informed Anglicans.

Celebrate Anglicanism is divided into seven chapters. It encourages use by groups — classes — where together inquirers can discover the treasure that is the Christian Faith in the Anglican Way. There are lots of questions to connect what is being learned to personal reflection or group discussion. The appendices offer everything from the classic creeds to a Church Constitution to contemporary statements from global gatherings.

Celebrate Anglicanism is particularly useful in describing the way in which historic and global Anglicanism has been recovered and renewed in the Anglican Church in North America. Indeed, the book helps one understand how the emergence of the Anglican Church in North America is the fruit of a world-wide Reformation of Anglicanism. Among the stories that are told is how the Global Anglican Future Conference of 2008 called for the foundation of the Anglican Church in North America as part of the re-centering of world-wide Anglicanism on the "Faith once for all delivered to the saints." The second Global Anglican Future Conference has met (2013) where the North American Province took its place as part of the great missionary movement, which is 21st century orthodox Anglicanism.

As one whose ministry has been concerned to offer the fullness of

Anglicanism as a very reliable way to invite, form, disciple and deploy committed Christians, I commend Celebrate Anglicanism to those who are looking for new life in Christ, and to those who are charged with preparing souls for such a life in the Anglican Way.

The Most Reverend Robert Duncan, D.D.
Archbishop of the Anglican Church in North America
Bishop of the Anglican Diocese of Pittsburgh

Preface

Celebrate Anglicanism addresses what I believe to be two of the most pressing questions facing the Anglican Church in North America.

First, what does it mean to be an Anglican? Most Anglicans in the United States are relatively new to the Anglican Church in North America. Even those who had been longtime members of the Episcopal Church have had little or no teaching about Anglicanism. A need exists, then, to establish a foundation for what it means to be an Anglican.

Second, what do I personally love about the Anglican Church? If we are to be successful church planters and to increase membership in our local parishes, we must all be able to tell our friends, neighbors, family, and coworkers what we personally love about the Anglican Church. Every member of every parish must be able to respond easily and comfortably to both questions.

Our journey will prepare us to *Celebrate Anglicanism* as we learn about:

- What it means to be an Anglican
- Basics of Apostolic Christianity
- Historical development of the Anglican Church
- Anglican doctrine, beliefs, and traditions
- Anglican liturgy
- The Anglican Communion
- The role of the laity in the Anglican Church
- The *Jerusalem Declaration*

Notice that Session One is rather long compared to the rest of the sessions. It is the longest session as it covers essential information about Apostolic Christianity as received from the apostles. It is important for all of us to understand the basics of Apostolic Christianity and the fundamentals of the orthodox Anglican Church. Be patient, but be committed to reading and learning as you start your journey.

Acknowledgments

It would be impossible to list all who have assisted me one way or another in completing *Celebrate Anglicanism*, but I am compelled to mention several individuals who have been extra special in their support and assistance and who took the time to review this manuscript.

Bishop Bill Thompson for his insight into the importance of the project to the Diocese of Western Anglicans, his prayer support, and his suggestions for improvement.

Bishop Terry Kelshaw for supporting this endeavor, and for urging me on with words of wisdom, encouragement, and prayer support.

Rev. Canon Dr. Michael Green for his support and suggestions for improvement.

Rev. Dr. Greg Peters for his support and suggestions for improvement.

Canon Ron Speers for supporting this book; for his patience, editing assistance, guidance in publishing, and prayer; and for being a brother in Christ to the end.

Canon Frank Trane, who was from the very beginning always available for discussion and provided many valuable suggestions.

The following are special folks who were supportive and helpful in a number of ways.

Rev. Pete and Julie Forbes, Rev. Brian and Laurin Capanna,

Rick and Connie Crossley, Kristen Davis Shumway, and Aimee Davis.

My Wednesday Morning Men's Group, who listened to more about *Celebrate Anglicanism* than ever should have been necessary.

Introduction

The Vision

A few years ago I attended a Christian men's weekend. It was a wonderful time of being together with other Anglican men, worshipping the Lord in song and prayer. Much of our teaching for the weekend dealt with discipleship. It started me thinking about discipleship training in our congregations, the lack of growth being experienced by many churches, and about planting new churches.

On Saturday night of the weekend, the men had an opportunity to receive prayer for their needs. During that time of prayer I had a vision. I rarely have visions, and sometimes I wonder about those who do, but I had one, and it was very clear. I saw a long line of faces passing before my eyes. The faces had no real definition and were gray in color. They were looking not at me but up into the sky, and they just kept coming and coming. They seemed lost. At the end of the prayer time I shared my vision with the young priest who had prayed with me. It seemed clear to us that these were the faces of the lost and they were looking for someone who would bring them the good news of Jesus Christ and hope for their lost lives. It was clarification for me that God had his hand on my *Celebrate Anglicanism* endeavor.

Most members of the Anglican Church in the United States are relative newcomers to the Anglican tradition. That being the case, if we are to reach out to the unsaved and the lost, it is imperative that we all have a firm grasp of what it means to be an Anglican.

If we are to expand membership in our local parishes, every member of every parish be able to respond to questions like "What is an Anglican?," "How has the Anglican Church helped you strengthen your faith in our Lord and Savior Jesus Christ?," and "What is the history of the Anglican Church?" This seven-week journey is designed to provide the basic information to prepare parish members to successfully reach out and share their faith and love of the Anglican Church with others.

The new Anglican province, the Anglican Church in North America (ACNA), is part of a second Great Reformation of the Church. We are being called to defend the orthodox faith as given to us by our early church fathers. We cannot let the secular-progressive society overrun our church.

> We are being called to defend the orthodox faith as given to us by our early church fathers.

Always being prepared to make a defense to anyone who asks you for a reason for the hope that is in you; yet do it with gentleness and respect. (1 Peter 3:15 ESV)

It is therefore critical to successfully defending our faith that we understand what we believe and who we are as Anglicans.

What a perfect time to *Celebrate Anglicanism*.

How to Best Use This Book

The purpose of *Celebrate Anglicanism* is to provide a seven-week study of the fundamentals of Apostolic Christianity and the history and traditions of the Anglican Church. This book may be used by small groups or by an individual desiring to learn about the Anglican strand of Apostolic Christianity.

Each session is in three parts: Information, Questions for Preparation, and Questions for Discussion.

Information

Each session will have material to read and study. Individuals may wish to research some of the topics or issues for better understanding, and that is most appropriate.

Questions for Preparation

Questions for Preparation are designed to provide an opportunity to think about, pray about, and prepare for small group meetings. Researching topics here is also appropriate.

Questions for Discussion

Questions for Discussion are to be used in the small group meetings or by an individual completing a self-study.

At the end of each week's study you will find the Questions for Preparation and Questions for Discussion. They will help guide you in your own preparation for celebrating Anglicanism. I suggest that you write out your responses in a notebook to help ensure that you have sufficient detail for each answer. Before you start answering the questions, pray first for guidance and wisdom, a point made clear by James, a brother of Jesus.

If any of you lacks wisdom, he should ask God, who gives generously to all without finding fault, and it will be given to him. (James 1:5)

Read and think about each question, taking whatever time is necessary (maybe even a day or two) to really think through your answers, and then answer in as much detail as you can. The questions are not all-inclusive, but they do reflect the areas of interest of many people concerning the Anglican Church. For some, the answers may come quickly, but for others it may take further prayer and even a little research. The "why" part of your answers may be difficult, but keep in mind that the "why" part is the most important thing that you'll be sharing with others who are seeking the truth about God for themselves.

Your words about God and His Church may be the most important words that someone will ever hear!

You'll notice that Session One is rather long compared to the rest of the sessions. It's the longest session because it covers essential information about Apostolic Christianity as received from the Apostles. It is important for all of us to understand the basics of Apostolic Christianity and the fundamentals of the orthodox Anglican Church. Be patient, but be committed to reading and learning as you start your journey.

Helpful Recommendations

Acquiring a three-ring or a spiral-bound notebook will be helpful. You will be asked to write responses to Questions for Preparation and Questions for Discussion at the end of each session. In addition there will be an opportunity to write several personal reflections. If you are in a small group discussion you might want to use your notebook to jot down thoughts or new insights during the discussion sessions.

Should a group or individual desire more in-depth information on a topic, there is a list of recommended readings in Appendix F.

If a congregation or parish desires to use small groups for this series, it is important for the group leader or facilitator to review Secrets for Group Leaders located in Appendix H prior to beginning this study. Following the suggested guidelines in Secrets will greatly facilitate a fun and productive small group.

It is recommended that clergy develop sermons based upon the teachings or concepts of each weekly session, starting with an introduction to the purpose or goal of the seven-week journey for your parish.

Session One

Leaving Our Nets

The Apostle Mark in his Gospel writes the words of Jesus that make clear what business we are in as Christians.

"Come, follow me," Jesus said, "and I will make you fishers of men." At once they left their nets and followed him. (Mark 1:17-18)

The part often forgotten is, "At once they left their nets and followed Him."

As Christians we do not have a problem accepting Christ as our Savior, but many of us are reluctant to leave our nets and follow Him; reluctant, meaning that we are hesitant or unwilling to do something contrary to our normal way of thinking. Savior, yes; Lord of our lives, not so much.

I believe there are two steps we can take to overcome our reluctance. First, we must personally make the decision to accept Jesus as our Lord and Savior. That is doable. No doubt you've already done so or you probably wouldn't be reading this. The second step is where problems seem to enter into the equation. To follow Jesus means to learn about Him, and then to go out and share what we have learned with others. For Anglicans to be successful in doing so, we must be well anchored in our Christian faith and have a solid understanding of the Anglican Church. Having both parts in place will not only enable us but will also *motivate* us to share our Christian faith and Anglicanism with others. What was seen as a difficult task now becomes a joyful opportunity to help the Lord build His kingdom.

Calling the Twelve

Jesus called twelve men to be his disciples. They spent three years listening to His teachings, watching Him, and seeing Him perform miracles. Jesus was preparing them for the time when they would be sent into the world to teach and share the gospel. In the meantime, they were learning and growing in knowledge of Him. Learning and growing is just as important for you and me as it was for the disciples 2000 years ago. (Always remember that you don't have to have learned *everything* before you should begin sharing what you have learned with others!)

The word *apostle* comes from the Greek word *apostolos*, which means *one sent with a special mission*. The Apostles were those sent out as teachers and ambassadors for Christ.

The Apostle Paul relates it this way:

> We are therefore Christ's ambassadors, as though God were making his appeal through us. (2 Corinthians 5:20)

Keep in mind that the word *apostle* was a term applied to the disciples selected by Jesus himself. The title *apostle* was extended only to select others like Paul and some early missionaries who were active in proclaiming the Gospel during the first generation of the church leadership, which is also known as the Apostolic Age. The point is that we are not and cannot become Apostles. However, we are called to become disciples sent out like the Apostles of the early church to teach the good news and make disciples of all men.* In fact, from the very beginning that is exactly what Jesus commanded for you and me.

Jesus first calls us, and then He commissions us:

> "Come, follow me," Jesus said, "and I will make you fishers of men." (Matt 4:19; Mark 1:17)

> "…and you will be my witnesses in Jerusalem, and in all Judea and Samaria, to the ends of the earth." (Acts 1:8)

---

*"Men" in this case (Matthew 4:19), of course, means both men and women. The Greek word here means *mankind, male and female*. The Message (MSG) paraphrased Bible says it this way: "Walking along the beach of Lake Galilee, Jesus saw two brothers: Simon (later called Peter) and Andrew. They were fishing, throwing their nets into the lake. It was their regular work. Jesus said to them, 'Come with me. I'll make a new kind of fisherman out of you. I'll show you how to catch men and women instead of perch and bass.' They didn't ask questions, but simply dropped their nets and followed."

For us, discipleship necessarily includes both *training* and *deployment*. In today's terms that means becoming an effective ambassador for Christ in our modern world by spreading the good news of the Gospel.

> For us, discipleship necessarily includes both *training* and *deployment.*

To be a disciple (trained and deployed) requires time and commitment. Our personal needs, family life, and work all take our time. Little time is left for growing in our faith, or so it seems. To accept the premise that we do not have time for study simply shows that our priorities are misplaced. In addition to having no time to devote to learning and growing, typical church members also tend to believe they are not capable of being effective ambassadors for Christ. As an example, a lady (I will call her Judy) in our Bible study had a close friend who was very sick. Judy wanted to pray for healing for her friend. Judy's biggest concern was how to go about witnessing to her friend, who was not yet a Christian. This seemed to be a daunting task for her. After some sharing and prayer, she was convinced that she must pray with her friend, and she did. The good news is that by Judy's reaching out in faith, her friend was given the opportunity to hear of God's love for her.

Sharing the Good News

The fact is, God wants us to be excited about being Christians and He commands us to share that excitement with others. He wants us to *celebrate* our Christianity every day at home, at work, and on the street. When we think about all God has done for us and is doing for us, we should indeed be thankful, grateful, humble, and excited about sharing the good news of Jesus Christ with others.

Think about church on Sunday morning. Do you walk out of church excited, or do you walk out of church and leave your spiritual enthusiasm behind? At the end of the service (or Dismissal), these words are spoken: "Go in peace to love and serve the Lord." Do we keep those words in our hearts and minds as we go out into the world? Do we love and serve the Lord? Or do we sort of forget the "serve" part? The Rt. Rev. Terry Kelshaw, a retired bishop and seminary professor, told our congregation that we should mount a sign over our exit doors at the back of our church reading **"Servants' Entrance"**! What a perfect reminder that we are all to go out into the world to serve the Lord.

The Church has developed excellent classes, weekend retreats, special programs, and sermons to help equip the laity. Even so, many members remain hesitant to get involved in sharing their love of the Lord. Most of us still do not carry the good news to others. I can remember finishing a conversation with a friend and later thinking I had passed up an opportunity to share Jesus with him. I asked myself why I was so hesitant to share about Jesus. Maybe you have had a similar experience in your life.

Secret disciples are a liability to the Christian cause.

The world-renowned evangelist and Oxford professor the Rev. Canon Dr. Michael Green makes a statement in his Christian Foundations course that really hits home: "Secret disciples are a liability to the Christian cause." We must not keep our Christianity to ourselves; it must be shared with others. Matthew quotes the words of Jesus that make our responsibility as a follower of Christ very clear:

> Neither do people light a lamp and put it under a bowl. Instead they put it on its stand, and it gives light to everyone in the house. In the same way, let your light shine before men, that they may see your good deeds and praise your Father in Heaven. (Matthew 5:15-16)

I am reminded of the Christian song that says, "This little light of mine, I'm gonna let it shine, let it shine, let it shine, let it shine." Do we let our little light shine for Jesus? It is a neat little song, but notice it says this "little" light of mine; not a huge beacon, but a little light. That's all we need to do to spread the good news of the Gospel to another person: just let our little light shine.

Discipleship is not a program; rather, it is a process! You might think of it as training followed by deployment. An important point to remember is that as a Christian, the training never stops and deployment should never cease. As we gain knowledge, our faith becomes stronger and our love of Jesus becomes greater. No matter where we are in our personal journey as Christians, we should be increasingly thankful, grateful, humble, and excited about what God has done and is continuing to do for us each and every day.

Lay Ministry in the Church

Our new province, the Anglican Church in North America (ACNA), has a straightforward, biblically based constitution and a refreshing set of canons (bylaws for a church) that are our defining guidelines. Canon 10 makes a very clear statement regarding the role of a layperson in today's church. Here is a portion of ACNA's Godly commissioning of the laity taken from Canon 10:

> The effective ministry of the Church is the responsibility of the laity no less than it is the responsibility of the bishop, priests and deacons. It is incumbent for every lay member of the Church to become an effective minister of the Gospel of Jesus Christ, one who is spiritually qualified, gifted, called, and mature in the faith.

Notice the last sentence, which deals with every lay member of the Church. We cannot escape the fact that each one of us has the responsibility, as a member of the Anglican Church, to be an effective minister of the Gospel of Jesus Christ. Our marching orders are clear.

God's Action Plan

The duties and responsibilities of each and every lay person (that means you and me) include continuing our instruction in the Faith so we can remain effective ministers of Jesus Christ among those who do not know Him.[1]

Matthew's Gospel contains the Great Commission that makes perfectly clear what we are called to do as Christians.

> Go therefore and make disciples of all nations, baptizing them in the name of the Father, and of the Son and of the Holy Spirit, teaching them to obey everything that I have commanded you. And surely, I am with you always, to the end of the age. (Matthew 28:19-20)

All of us who are baptized Christians are supposed to be disciples (effective *learners* and *ambassadors*) for Christ. So why is it so difficult for us to be successful in both areas? Well, as it turns out, we're not unique in this regard. Think about the first disciples who later became the Apostles. They were in intensive training for three years and still they didn't seem to really understand what the Lord was teaching them. The key to their eventual success was the infilling of the Holy Spirit after Jesus departed from them.

The Apostle Luke records this in Jesus' own corollary to the Great Commission:

> But you will receive power when the Holy Spirit comes upon you; and you will be my witnesses in Jerusalem, and in all Judea and Samaria, and to the ends of the earth. (Acts 1:8)

Jesus is telling his disciples that they must go and share Gospel with the entire world! By the power of the Holy Spirit they will fulfill the Great Commission. The same is true for you and me! Let's say that again: The same is true for you and me. When we choose to release the Holy Spirit, who dwells within us, to work actively in our hearts, we are empowered to do what Christ has commanded us to do. Christians in the 21st century are empowered by the Holy Spirit just as the Apostles were empowered at Pentecost (Acts 2:1-31) to fulfill the Great Commission. That is because "Jesus Christ is the same yesterday and today and forever" (Hebrews 13:8).

Finding Our Direction

Once we discern God's purpose for our life, we can become incredible ambassadors for Christ.

Dr. Sheri Benvenuti, a pastor and missionary and a professor at Vanguard University, explains that when we are filled with the Holy Spirit, we are able to find out or discern who it is that God created us to be and what it is that we are to do for Him. Once we discern God's purpose for our life, we can become incredible ambassadors for Christ. The Holy Spirit is patiently awaiting the opportunity to be our director, guide, and source of spiritual power to share the good news of Jesus Christ with others. Of course we must seek to allow the Holy Spirit to work within us and empower us to successfully do the Lord's work. The Holy Spirit (or Holy Ghost) is not just any spiritual force; He is the third person of the Trinity who proceeds from the Father and the Son and is not separated from either of them (John 14:26; Nicene Creed; Apostles' Creed).

Empowered by the Holy Spirit

Can you imagine what the Apostles experienced when they were empowered by the Holy Spirit and commissioned to go forth to share the Good News with the world? These were simple men who were certainly not trained evangelists or priests. They had spent three years traveling with Jesus, observing him, listening to His teachings, and asking questions. During those years, they were in a learning mode. They were not sent out on their historic world-changing mission until they received the power of the Holy Spirit. Luke writes in his Gospel the words of Jesus:

> I am going to send you what my Father has promised; but stay
> in the city until you have been clothed with power from on high.
> (Luke 24:49)

Jesus had selected those who would be His disciples from among a wide variety of men. He knew they would be successful when they received the power of the Holy Spirit. He also knew the kind of lifestyles they would exhibit as Apostles after the infilling of the Holy Spirit. If we could define those lifestyles, we might well find a good model for ourselves in terms of what others see in us.

Christian Lifestyle Traits

Certainly there was something about the Apostles that made them stand out. Michael Green has suggested what an authentic Christian lifestyle might look like to outsiders. He lists the stable qualities or lifestyle traits[2] that were visible in the lives of the Apostles and other early Christians as recorded in the Book of Acts.

Dedication	Completed tasks given to them by the Lord
Enthusiasm	Had a sincere desire to spread the Good News
Joy	Maintained a joyful outlook even in the tough times
Faith	Had a strong and unwavering faith in the Lord
Endurance	Did what needed to be done
Holiness	Lived in peace, freedom, and purity without offending others
Spiritual Power	Were enabled by the power of the Spirit to do God's work
Courage	Went into society spreading the Gospel without hesitation
Generosity	Provided a helping hand to others who were in need
Prayer	Maintained a strong and committed prayer life
Transformation	Lived positive lifestyles attractive to non-believers

Michael Green concludes that the Apostle's lifestyles as revealed in the Book of Acts reminded people of Jesus. Such is the action of the Holy Spirit, for as Jesus said, "He will bring glory to me by taking from what is mine and making it known to you" (John 16:14).

> When they saw the courage of Peter and John and realized that they were unschooled, ordinary men, they were astonished and they took note that these men had been with Jesus. (Acts 4:13)

As Christians, we should strive to reflect the Apostles' lifestyle traits in our lives. Check your own lifestyle traits against the list above, then list three that you would need to strengthen in order for you to live a more effective Christian lifestyle on a day-to-day basis.

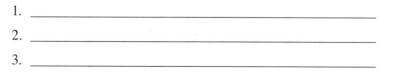

1. _____

2. _____

3. _____

Personal Reflection

Take a moment to reflect on each of the lifestyle traits you selected. Pray for the Lord's direction as to what you must do to strengthen each one. Record in your notebook the action steps necessary for you to strengthen each lifestyle trait on your list.

The lifestyle characteristics of a Christian disciple may seem to be pretty unattainable. It may seem to us that we can never be like the Apostles, but we all need to give it a go. Jesus said in John's Gospel:

> If you remain in me, and my words remain in you, ask whatever you wish, and it will be given you. This is my Father's glory, that you bear much fruit, showing yourselves to be my disciples. (John 15: 7-8)

It's perfectly clear that Jesus wants us not merely to be faithful followers, but to be disciples who will function as ambassadors to spread the Gospel. Remember, we're talking about both training and deployment. That may be news for some; but remember that His yoke is easy and His burden is light.

Celebrate Anglicanism

Okay, how do we *Celebrate Anglicanism*? To celebrate means to mark something with respect, festivity, or rejoicing; to extol or praise it; and to display it and make it widely known.

Take a moment and list five reasons why you are an Anglican. Feel free to record your list in your notebook if you need more space.

1. _____
2. _____
3. _____
4. _____
5. _____

I decided to ask a number of people, both newcomers and longtime members of the church, what questions they would like to ask about the Anglican Church. Some of the responses were surprising, but all were interesting, and they covered a wide range of topics. Here are some examples of questions submitted by the participants in my little survey: [3]

- Is the Anglican Church a Christian church?
- Can't I just love Jesus and not attend church?
- What is all the stuff around the altar?
- Is the Anglican Church only for folks over the age of 40?
- What's with all the outfits the priest wears?
- Do you believe mostly the Old Testament or the New Testament?
- Why are some Anglicans always crossing themselves?

Well, you get the point. There is a real marketplace for the knowledge we'll be acquiring in our journey. The reason is simple: We need to know about our church before we can settle in on what we love about it.

I would like to answer the question above relating to age. You do not have to be 40 years old to be an Anglican! There is no minimum, and, for that matter, no maximum age limit. You are accepted and loved by the Anglican Church at any age.

Please know that not all questions on the list will be answered here, but do bring up any questions you might have in your small group or with your rector or pastor.

What We Like About our Anglican Church

I also asked a number of Anglican friends what they liked about the Anglican Church. Here are some of their answers:

- Traditions
- Daily Offices (Morning Prayer, Evening Prayer)
- Liturgy
- Lots of involvement of the congregation in the church services
- Book of Common Prayer (BCP)*
- The Church's desire to be Christlike
- Treats members like mature adults
- The Apostolic succession

---

*The Book of Common Prayer (BCP) was first published in 1549. The prayer book provides structure to services of worship, which Anglicans refer to as *liturgy*. A significant revision to the BCP, published in 1662, became, and still is, the official prayer book of the Church of England. Of several revisions made to the BCP in the United States, the 1928 and 1979 versions have been the most commonly been used by Anglican Church in North America. In 2013 the College of Bishops of the ACNA approved and published *Texts for Common Prayer* along with The Ordinal. As "working texts" churches have an opportunity to experience the rites and provide feedback to the House of Bishops prior to the new prayer book being finalized.

These short and easy answers became more interesting when I asked my friends to explain their answers, to give the "why." It suddenly got real quiet. Finally one person said, "I need some time to think about my response." That honest answer illustrates that most of us will need to take some time to develop our own answers more fully.

I had written down, **"I am excited about being an Anglican because I love and appreciate the liturgy."**

Well, what does that really mean?

Why do I love and appreciate the liturgy?

Why would someone be motivated to come to church just to experience what I consider to be the beauty of the liturgy without a more complete explanation?

Okay, here goes; here's the "why" of my answer. The Anglican liturgy is taken from the Bible and reflects what Christ himself commanded us to do as a congregation. Our liturgy is centered on God and permits us to worship God in a way he has intended. The word liturgy is from the Greek *leitourgia*, which means "participation of the people in the work of God." Our liturgy is one in which the whole congregation participates.

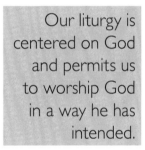

Our liturgy is centered on God and permits us to worship God in a way he has intended.

I love our liturgy because it provides order and a sequence to our church service. Whenever I attend another Anglican Church I feel at home and comfortable, because I know and understand the order of service. The liturgy reminds me of the great traditions of the Early Church that we have had from the beginning. We celebrate the Lord's Supper in the same way He did in the upper room and as He has commanded us to do until his return. For me, the liturgy of the Eucharist leads me to a time and place where I know I am in His presence, my faith is strengthened, and I experience a heightened love of Christ in my heart.

That may not be your answer, but you should take the time to know exactly why you love the Anglican Church. Writing your Personal Refection should be challenging and exciting at the same time.

Personal Reflection

Take some time and write your personal response to the question, "Why do I love the Anglican Church?"

The excitement of our time is that God has privileged you and me to be part of a second Great Reformation of His Church, not unlike the Great Reformation five hundred years ago. Ours is a time when our commitment to the Lord needs to be ever stronger. It is critical that each of us has a solid understanding as to why we love our Anglican portion of Christ's Church and why we are excited about what God is doing in our home parishes to build His Kingdom!

> God has privileged you and me to be part of a second Great Reformation of His Church.

Each and every one of us needs to be ready and able to share a Godly sense of excitement with our family, friends, and neighbors, wherever and whenever we are led by the Holy Spirit to do so. For this reason the Apostle Peter exhorts us:

> Always be prepared to give an answer to everyone who asks you to give a reason for the hope that you have. But do this in gentleness and respect, keeping a clear conscience, so that those who speak maliciously against your good behavior in Christ may be ashamed of their slander. (1 Peter 3:15-16)

Catechesis, the Basics of Faith

Catechesis is a fancy word meaning to receive instruction in the basic doctrines of Christianity. As we begin our study of Anglicanism it is important for us to all be working with the same knowledge base. With that in mind, we will review three foundational tenets of Christianity that are very important to understand: The Holy Trinity, the ministry of the Holy Spirit, and the importance of the Cross to Christians.

What is the Holy Trinity?

It is a fundamental Christian doctrine that God is a triune God, existing as three persons, but one God. It may be hard to understand, but as Christians, by faith, we believe it. Let us look at what the historical documents of the church have to say about the Holy Trinity.

The Creed of Saint Athanasius has been accepted and adopted by Christian churches since the sixth century. Together, the Nicene Creed, the Apostles' Creed, and the Athanasian Creed form the creedal foundation of Anglicanism. The three creeds can found in Appendix A, B, and C. The Creed of Saint Athanasius is an official statement of Christian doctrine, principally in regard to the Holy Trinity and the incarnation, and was probably composed during the life of St. Athanasius (d. 373) but not actually by him. It can be found in the 1979 Book of Common Prayer as a historical document of the church, and also in Appendix B of this book. In part the creed states:

> So there is one Father, not three Fathers; one Son, not three Sons; one Holy Ghost, not three Holy Ghosts. And in this Trinity none is afore, or after another; none is greater, or less than another; But the whole three Persons are coeternal together, and coequal. So that in all things, as aforesaid, the Unity in Trinity, and the Trinity in Unity are to be worshipped. He therefore that will be saved must thus think of the Trinity. (1979 BCP, 864)

Turn to Appendix B and read the creed carefully. It tells you who Jesus and the Trinity are in an indelible fashion. It will teach you that Jesus, by his incarnation, became man and that He is and remains, at one and the same time, all God and all man.

You may find it difficult to comprehend how three persons can be a single person as well. Perhaps a simple (and of course imperfect) illustration from nature may help us visualize the three-in-one nature of the Holy Trinity. Suppose the sun represents God. If its ball represents the Father, then the rays that radiate from the sun and create light for the world represent Jesus, and the warmth we feel, but cannot see, is the Holy Spirit.

Well, this certainly isn't proper theology, but if it helps anyone to get past a sticking point about the Trinity, then perhaps it's useful. Of course, God isn't up in the sky; He is omnipresent and lives within believers.

The figure below is called the "Shield of the Trinity." It is a visual representation of the relationships in the Holy Trinity. The origin of this diagram is unknown, but it dates to the early 1100s. Its most widespread use was during the 15th and 16th centuries, and it can be found as part of stained-glass windows and ornamental carvings in a number of churches in England. Do spend a few moments really absorbing it.

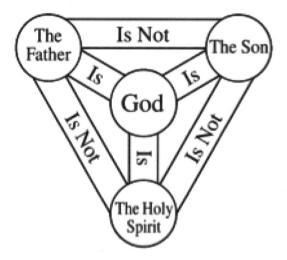

The Ministry of the Holy Spirit

We often hear about the Holy Spirit, yet we might not understand how He operates in our daily lives. The late John Stott (1921-2011), a renowned British Anglican priest and leader in the worldwide evangelical movement, gave a very practical example of how the Holy Spirit operates in believers. He developed what he called the "5-D" formula, or "the five steps or stages in the sanctifying activity of the Holy Spirit."[4]

According to Stott's 5-D formula, the Holy Spirit operates in:

1. Our **mind**, enabling us to **D**iscern the will of God

2. Our **conscience**, enabling us to **D**istinguish right and wrong

3. Our **heart**, enabling us to **D**esire God's way ardently

4. Our **will**, enabling us to **D**etermine resolutely to do God's will

5. And in so doing, he enables us to **D**o as He directs us

Although the steps may seem rather obvious, they can only occur when we choose to surrender our own will and permit the power of the Holy Spirit to operate within us.

Why Is the Cross Important?

The Cross is at the core of Christianity. Without the crucifixion of Christ and the fact that He rose from the dead, we would not have the assurance of eternal life. Jesus would be just another good man. As the Apostle Paul so clearly stated:

> If Christ has not been raised, then our preaching is useless and so is your faith is in vain...And if Christ has not been raised, your faith is futile and you are still in your sins...If only in Christ we have hope in this life, we are to be pitied more than all men. (1 Corinthians 15:14, 17, 19 ESV)

John Stott summarized the importance of the cross this way:

> Sin caused an estrangement; the cross, the crucifixion of Christ, has accomplished an atonement. Sin bred enmity; the cross-brought peace. Sin created a gulf between man and God; the cross has bridged it. Sin broke the fellowship; the cross-restored it. The cross is the symbol of our faith. Christian faith is the faith of Christ crucified.[5]

Keep in mind that only a perfectly righteous person could die as a sacrifice for another's sin. God loved us so much that he sent His Son Jesus, who is the **only** perfectly righteous person, to die for our sins. In his Gospel the Apostle John records Jesus' very own words about the Cross in this well-known passage:

Keep in mind that only a perfectly righteous person could die as a sacrifice for another's sin.

35

> For God so loved the world that he gave his one and only Son, that whoever believes in him shall not perish but have eternal life. (John 3:16)

Jesus loved us so much that He was willing to suffer and die in our place for our sin. On the cross Jesus took on our sin, and we received His righteousness.

God made Him who had no sin to be sin for us, so that in Him we might become the righteousness of God. (2 Corinthians 5:21)

Although we were under the penalty of death for our sin—"For the wages of sin is death, but the free gift of God is eternal life in Christ Jesus our Lord" (Romans 6:23)— a divine exchange occurred when Jesus suffered the penalty for our sin that we might receive the blessings that He deserved for living a sinless life.

God who judges sin now declares believers "not guilty." That is, God expunges the record of it so as to remember our sin no more.

> For this is the [new] covenant that I will make with the house of Israel after those days, declares the Lord...I will forgive their iniquity, and I will remember their sin no more. (Jeremiah 31:33-34)
> ...and the blood of Jesus cleanses us from all sin. (1 John 1:7 ESV)

This is incredibly good news for us!

It gets even richer for believers because, even though we have been forgiven and made the righteous of God in Christ, we are still in a learning mode and prone to miss the mark; yet, as the Apostle John reminds us:

> If we confess our sins, he is faithful and just to forgive us our sins and to cleanse us from all unrighteousness. (1 John 1:9 ESV)

So instead of running *from* Jesus when we sin, we should always run *to* him when we sin!

You will no doubt see a number of crosses in Anglican churches, most often the resurrection cross that does not depict the body of Christ on it. It is an empty cross with deep spiritual meaning, reminding us that indeed Christ did rise from the grave, while at the same time reminding us that he died on the cross for our sins. Christ's suffering on the cross bridged the gap between sinful man and a holy God. His death and resurrection make new life possible for all who believe in Him.

> For there is one God, and there is one mediator between God and men, the man Christ Jesus who gave himself as a ransom for all men, the testimony given in its proper time. (1 Timothy 2:5)

The Anglican Church in North America (ACNA) has just released a new Catechism entitled: *To Be a Christian: An Anglican Catechism*. The Catechism was unanimously approved January 8, 2014, for use by the ACNA College of Bishops.

The authors describe the Catechism as, "designed to make clear to everyone what it means to be a Christian. It will open to you the door to knowing Jesus Christ and experiencing the full love of God through him. It will lead to the full involvement in the life and mission of the Church, as you become a citizen of the Kingdom of God. It will further anchor you in the full reality of unquenchable joy, beginning in this life and ever increasing in the life to come."

This book is an outstanding reference and may be used for in-depth study of our Apostolic Christian faith. The question-and-answer format allows for easy learning and small group discussion. *To Be a Christian: An Anglican Catechism* is a must have for all those exploring Christianity and our Apostolic Christian Faith. Visit the ACNA web site (www. anglicanchurch.net) for information on how to secure a copy.

Session One has been rather long. It contains a lot of information, but it is important information that we as Anglicans need to know and understand in order to become effective ambassadors for Christ.

It's now time to dig a little deeper by completing the Questions for Preparation and Discussion.

Session One
Questions for Preparation and Discussion

Questions for Preparation

1. What do you see as the importance of the Creed of Saint Athanasius to the Christian Church?

2. John Stott developed what he calls the "5-D" formula that he defined as "the five steps or stages in the sanctifying activity of the Holy Spirit." Which of the steps is the most difficult for you? Explain your answer.

3. Why is Christ the only person able to die on the cross as an acceptable sacrifice for our sins?

4. Explain the Holy Trinity in your own words.

Questions for Discussion

1. It has been said that Christ's suffering on the cross bridged the gap between sinful man and a Holy God. What do you understand that statement to mean?

2. The Apostle John records the last three words that Jesus uttered before His death when He said, "It is finished" (John 19:30). What do His final three words mean to you? How would you explain them to others?

3. What do you think the Apostles experienced when they were first empowered by the Holy Spirit?

Session Two

What Is an Anglican?

Recently my wife and I had an exceptional experience when praying for a woman we had never met before and haven't seen since. Who was she? An angel? Perhaps. But her simple question was the real impetus behind *Celebrate Anglicanism*.

"What is an *An-gel-i-can*?"

An-gel-i-can? I was speechless, and then I almost laughed out loud. All that came to mind in answer to her question were Hollywood movies I'd seen on television about King Henry VIII and his keen interest in wives. The films were entertaining, but they lacked accurate historical information concerning the Church of England.

What would have been an appropriate answer?

I was surprised at my lack of knowledge about my own church. What *is* an Anglican? I had some work to do.

The more I have learned about the Anglican Church, the more I have come to love what she stands for as representing authentic, historic Christianity.

This second week of our study we will define some basic terms and learn some fundamental information about the Anglican Church and we'll explore some pretty fascinating Anglican history. We'll also clear up some of the prevalent misconceptions about the Anglican Church.

What Is the Meaning of the Word Anglican?

The word *Anglican* originates from a medieval Latin phrase, *ecclesia anglicana*, which means the English Church. The term is used to describe those who believe in and follow the core beliefs and traditions of the Church of England. The English Church became the Church of England in 1534 when Parliament passed the Act of Supremacy, which declared King Henry VIII the Supreme Governor of the Church of England.

Is the Anglican Church a Christian Church?

Absolutely! Christianity is defined as the teachings and way of life made possible by the death, burial, and resurrection of Jesus Christ.[6] A Christian is one who believes in and is a follower of Jesus Christ as the Messiah.[7] The Anglican Church traces its roots to the Book of Acts and the Apostles' teachings. Hence, you may hear the term "the faith once for all delivered to the Saints." Oh yes, we are very Christian. Perhaps we could add that the Anglican Church represents authentic Christianity, *authentic* meaning *worthy of acceptance as conforming to the original* so as to reproduce its essential features; it's made or done the same way as the original.

> The Anglican Church traces its roots to the Book of Acts and the Apostles' teachings.

Is Anglicanism a Special Form of Christianity?

Geoffrey Francis Fisher, the 99th Archbishop of Canterbury from 1945 until 1961, famously said:

> The Anglican Communion has no peculiar thought, practice, creed, or confession of its own. It has only the Catholic Faith of the ancient Catholic Church, as preserved in the Catholic Creeds and maintained in the Catholic and Apostolic constitution of Christ's Church from the beginning. It is permitted to teach as necessary for salvation nothing but what is read in the Holy Scriptures as God's Word written or may be proved thereby. It therefore embraces and affirms such teachings of the ancient Fathers and Councils of the church as are agreeable to the Scriptures, and thus to be counted apostolic.

The Church has no authority to innovate: it is obliged continually, and particularly in times of renewal or reformation, to return to the faith once delivered to the saints. To be an Anglican, then, is not to embrace a distinct version of Christianity, but a distinct way of being a mere Christian, at the same time evangelical, apostolic, catholic, reformed, and Spirit-filled.[8]

The Rt. Rev. Jack Iker, Bishop of Ft. Worth, put it this way:

There is a basic fallacy in assuming that Anglicans are part of a denomination in the first place. We are not. We are members of the Catholic Church, not a denomination. I invite us all to look beyond the surface level of our Anglican identity, with its temptation to denominationalism, and go back to our heritage as catholic Christians … We are a fellowship within, or a branch of, the one holy catholic and apostolic Church, maintaining and propagating the faith and order of the historic Church throughout the ages. This means that we are not members of a sectarian, Protestant denomination, but of the Catholic Church … Remember, the Church of England, which came to be known as Anglican, existed before the Reformation.[9]

> We are members of the Catholic Church, not a denomination.

So the answer is **no,** Anglicanism is not a special form of Christianity. It is a preservation of authentic Christianity as given to the Apostles by our Lord and passed down to us through the generations. It has been said that Anglicanism is a container for Christian truth to pass along from one generation to another. That's pretty apt and should be one of your points to remember!

Personal Reflection

"Anglicanism is a container for the Apostolic Christian faith to be passed along from generation to generation." What does this statement mean to you as a 21st Century Christian?

What Do Anglicans Believe About God?

Anglicans, by faith and in agreement with all true Christians, understand and know that the Father, the Son, and the Holy Spirit comprise the Holy Trinity and define God.

Father   God is love, caring for creation and for every human being as His beloved children.

Son   God as He has revealed himself in the historical person of Jesus Christ, who is a real person alive today and who lives forever to make intercession for us. Jesus' life, death, resurrection, and ascension hold the key to knowing and loving God and making sense of life, before and after our death.

Holy Spirit   God is alive, loving, and active in the here and now, today, inspiring faith, justice, and truth, giving spiritual gifts to the church and guidance to His people for bearing good fruit in the world.

It has been aptly said that the Father chose us, the Son redeems us, and the Holy Spirit has sealed us forever.

Anglicans believe that Jesus Christ is more than just the Son of God: He is God the Son, the second person of the Holy Trinity. We understand the Apostles' Creed (1979 BCP, page 53) as the basic statement of Christian belief, the Nicene Creed (1979 BCP, page 326) as the sufficient statement of the Christian faith, and the Creed of St. Athanasius (1979 BCP, page 864) to be a sufficient statement of the nature of Jesus Christ and of the Holy Trinity. Anglicans are committed to perpetuating the faith "that was once for all delivered to the saints," as Jude, a servant of Jesus Christ and brother of James, exhorts all believers to do:

I felt I had to write and urge you to contend for the faith that was once for all entrusted to the saints. (Jude 1:3)

The Bible and the Anglican Church

Personal Reflection
How important is the Bible to you in your life?

How important is the Bible to Anglicans? The Word of God is the very heart of our Anglican identity!

Anglicans understand the Word of God as set forth in the Old and New Testaments of the Bible to contain all things necessary for salvation and to be the rule and ultimate standard for Christian living. In other words, the Bible is the anchor of our faith and everything is tied to it.

Archbishop Henry Luke Orombi of the Anglican Church of Uganda, writing on the importance of the Bible for the Anglican Church, states:

> The Bible is the anchor of our faith and everything is tied to it.

The Bible cannot appear to us a cadaver, merely to be dissected, analyzed, and critiqued, as has been the practice of much modern higher biblical criticism. Certainly we engage in biblical scholarship and criticism, but what is important to us is the power of the Word of God precisely as the Word of God—written to bring transformation in our lives, our families, our communities, and our culture. For us, the Bible is "living and active, sharper than a double-edged sword, it penetrates to dividing soul and spirits, joints and marrow, it judges the thoughts and attitudes of the heart" (Hebrews 4:12). The transforming effect of the Bible on Ugandans has generated so much conviction and confidence that believers were martyred in the defense of the message of salvation through Jesus Christ that it brought . . .

For all God's people, obedience to this Bible is the source of confidence, abundant life, and joy. It is an absolute treasure that no one can take away. Isaiah, later quoted by Peter, wrote, "The grass withers and the flowers fall, but the word of our God stands forever" (Isaiah 40:8).

The grass on which our cattle feed, the grass from which our roofs are thatched, all this withers. But the Word of God has withstood the test of time. The Bible is at the heart of our Anglican identity, and we Ugandan Anglicans joyfully submit to its life-giving and transforming authority."[10]

Is the Anglican Church an Episcopal Church?

The Anglican Church is not an **E**piscopal Church; it is an **e**piscopal church. We had better start by defining the small "e" word *episcopal*. It means *of or relating to a bishop or bishop's authority*. Thus a Christian denomination having bishops—for example, Anglican, Lutheran, and Methodist Churches—can be said to be episcopal with a small "e."

During the American Revolution, the Church of England parishes in the colonies were cut off from English ties and financial support. Soon after the war they adopted the name Episcopal (capital E) in order to distinguish themselves from the British crown and the Church of England. Simply put, it was good "marketing" at that time.

Through the years the Episcopal Church in the United States has been drifting ever farther away from biblical Christianity, with the result that it has been hemorrhaging congregations in fits and starts for many decades. For example, as early as 1873, in protest of increasing "Romanism" and departures from the Book of Common Prayer, a large group of congregations left the Episcopal Church to form the Reformed Episcopal Church, which is now a part of our new Anglican Church in North America (ACNA) province. Surges in disaffiliations from the Episcopal Church occurred in the 1970s and 1980s over changes to the Book of Common Prayer and the ordination of female priests, and again following the 2003 consecration of an openly gay noncelibate bishop.

At this writing, 22 of the 38 Anglican provinces worldwide have declared that they are either in impaired or broken communion with the Episcopal Church. Meanwhile, archbishops representing more than three-quarters of all Anglicans globally are in communion with ACNA.

What Is the Episcopate?

The *episcopate* means a bishop's office or his length of time in office, or it can mean the whole body of bishops taken together. Like the church of the earliest times, Anglicans do believe in oversight by a bishop. The chief work of the bishop is the propagation and defense of the faith and of Godly order as the visible sign and expression of the Church. Bishops are much more than governors; they are also the spiritual leaders of a diocese. It is important to realize that the offices of bishop, priest, and deacon were already in place in the Church by the mid-second century.

Archbishop Henry Orombi writes:

A bishop is consecrated in apostolic succession to be the apostolic presence in the community. A bishop, therefore, is the ongoing presence and voice of the apostles. He is our link to the early Church, and this link between bishop and the apostles (apostolicity) gives Anglicans our trans-cultural identity. The implication, therefore, is that the essence of Anglican identity is to be apostolic. More than a simple unbroken line of consecrations, we are to be apostolic in nature: faithful to the apostolic message, submitted to apostolic authority in Scripture, committed to apostolic mission and ministry, and devoted to apostolic worship.[11]

> A bishop is consecrated in apostolic succession to be the apostolic presence in the community.

The eminent British cleric The Rt. Rev. Dr. Bishop Michael Nazir-Ali heartily agrees:

Bishops are not just presiding Presbyters, but have a line of descent through apostolic delegates (Timothy & Titus) and prophets. In other words, episcopal office is not just about presiding, but also about mission and the prophetic.[12]

The Origins of the Anglican Church

Michael Green has encapsulated what should be our takeaway from a study of the history of the Anglican Church:

To get people to see that the Church in England goes back to earliest times and was not founded by Henry VIII, and to show them that it is just a container for apostolic faith and practice, could do massive good in this present time. This will have an invaluable educational effect among church people...who are normally ill-educated on such issues!"[13]

Let's take a closer look at the development of the Church in England.

The Earliest Beginnings in England

Although the new Anglican province in North America was founded as recently as 2009, the earliest roots of our Anglican heritage date to the Roman Empire's occupation of Britain. It is likely that Roman soldiers brought Christianity with them to Britain and that the church came into existence there around the year AD 43. The early Christian writers Tertullian (c. 155-220) and Origen (c. 185-254) mention the existence of a British church in the early third century. By the fourth century, British bishops were attending a number of the great councils of the Church. The first member of the British church whom we know by name is St. Alban. Tradition tells us he was martyred for his faith on the spot where St. Albans Abbey now stands in St. Albans, England.

What eventually became known as the Church of England was the result of a combination of three early streams of Christianity: 1) the Roman tradition of St. Augustine and his successors, 2) the remnants of the old Romano-British church, and 3) the Celtic tradition coming down from Scotland and associated with people like St. Aidan and St. Cuthbert.[14] For about a thousand years, until the Reformation in the 16th century, the Church in England acknowledged the authority of the Pope.

The Protestant Reformation

Well before Martin Luther posted his *Ninety-Five Theses* on the Castle Church door in Wittenburg, Germany, in 1517 (thus catalyzing the

Protestant Reformation of the 16th century), the Roman Catholic Church had become problematic, to say the least. Among the issues were the fact that the Roman church had become a major economic power; that it fostered the belief that there were middlemen to be employed if one sought to reach God; that God's favor could be purchased with money (the sale of indulgences); and a theology of guilt, shame, and works as necessary for salvation. The Roman church was clearly in need of reformation; that is, of returning to its Godly roots. The leadership of the Roman church had deserted the basic principles of the faith and had begun instituting rules as they desired.

The apostasy was great in spiritual matters, the church's sale of sin indulgencies for money being but one example. These and many other factors had eroded people's faith in the Roman Catholic Church and led to the Great Reformation or "Protestant Reformation" in the 16th century. This split within Western Christianity was initiated by Martin Luther, a Roman Catholic priest, and John Calvin, a French theologian. Another important reformer was Thomas Cranmer, the Archbishop of Canterbury during and following the reign of England's King Henry VIII.

Importantly, the Roman church had become the main economic power of the late middle ages. In England, for example, Roman Catholic monasteries controlled most of the usable land in an era when land was the main source of wealth. There is no doubting the fact that challenging the power and wealth of a bloated church was in the air in those days. King Henry VIII was riding a groundswell of change, a new day when monarchs in Europe were already contesting the Pope's authority and cutting the power of the Church down to size. Kings in Henry's day were rejecting papal supremacy and making their own decisions in church matters, resulting in the Pope losing influence in a number of countries. Sweden's King, for example, had taken control of the church there several years before Henry ever acted to sever relations with Rome.

The English Reformation

The idea that Henry VIII founded the Church of England is prevalent, but it is not true, since the Church in England predates Henry VIII by more than a thousand years. The Church in England existed from earliest times, although it received its specific identity as the Church of England at the time of the Great Reformation. So old Henry had nothing to do with founding the church, as antagonists like to claim. Perhaps an easy way to look at Anglicanism is to remember that the Church has been *in* England since Britain was a Roman Colony.

> The Church in England predates Henry VIII by more than a thousand years.

The Church *of* England resulted after England rejected the primacy of the Pope. The Church of England continued to be a part of the one, holy, catholic and apostolic Church, but without allegiance to the Pope or the superstructure of the Roman Catholic Church.

The point to remember is that in its structure, the English church remained as it always had been in everything except for obedience to the Pope, while other countries in Europe were becoming Lutheran or Calvinist. (Luther and Calvin actually established new churches, while Cranmer was left with a fully intact church, albeit one that was severed from Rome.)

It is important to note that Thomas Cranmer, who had earlier spent substantial time in Germany with the Protestant reformers, adopted the Protestant understanding that salvation is solely by the unmerited grace of God through faith in Jesus Christ. Cranmer gradually introduced this understanding into the English church in place of the medieval theology of salvation through guilt, shame, and works of repentance.

Henry asserted that his first marriage had never been valid, but the divorce issue (annulment, actually) was only one factor in Henry's desire to change the Church. He used the Church for power and wealth, too, as with his Dissolution of the Monasteries that amounted to expropriation of wealth for the royal coffers. But the English reformers, Archbishop Thomas Cranmer in particular, used the supreme power of the King to their advantage as well. In spiritual matters, where it counts, for example, the reformers instituted the Book of Common Prayer, the Books of Homilies, and the Articles of Religion.

King Henry VIII never formally repudiated the doctrines of the Roman Catholic Church, but he declared himself supreme head of the Church in England. This, combined with other subsequent actions, eventually resulted in the Church in England permanently separating from the Roman Catholic Church. It is not generally well understood that Henry's break with Rome was a gradual thing.

During 1536 and 1537 (before he was excommunicated by Rome in 1538), Henry instituted a number of statutes—the Act of Appeal, the Act of Succession, and the Act of Supremacy—that dealt with the relationship between the king, the pope, and the structure of the Church in England.

Henry's changes to the Church struck at the heart of its wealth and its relationship with the monarchy and involved more complex motives and methods than his desire for a new wife and an heir. He deserves credit for pursuing his policy skillfully and consistently, but definitely not for founding the Church of England.

Session Two
Questions for Preparation
and Discussion

Questions for Preparation

1. What is your understanding of the term *Anglicanism*?
2. How does the Anglican Church in North America relate to the Episcopal Church in the United States?
3. What does "the faith once for all delivered to the saints" mean to you?
4. What is the importance of the Bible to the Anglican Church?
5. What part did King Henry VIII play in the Reformation?
6. What is the role of a bishop in the Anglican Church?
7. How did the Church of England evolve differently from Protestant Churches on the European continent?

Questions for Discussion

1. Why did you decide to become an Anglican?
2. Why do you remain an Anglican?
3. In what ways is the Anglican Church a unique church?
4. If you had to describe Anglicanism in one word, what would that word be? Why?

Session Three

Anglican Beliefs, Doctrine, and Tradition

What do Anglicans believe? This question requires information on a number of key issues that include core beliefs, doctrine, traditions, and theology.

Anglican Core Beliefs

The founding entities of the Anglican Church in North America (ACNA), who came together in 2009, agreed to the Fundamental Declarations, a set of core Christian beliefs that are common among orthodox Anglicans around the world. My own Diocese of Western Anglicans refers to the core beliefs as a Statement of Faith. Member churches of ACNA must agree to the following core beliefs without exception: [15]

1. We confess the canonical books of the Old and New Testaments to be the inspired Word of God, containing all things necessary for salvation, and to be the final authority and unchangeable standard for Christian faith and life.

2. We confess Baptism and the Supper of the Lord to be Sacraments ordained by Christ Himself in the Gospel, and thus to be ministered with unfailing use of His words of institution and of the elements ordained by Him.

3. We confess the godly historic Episcopate as an inherent part of the apostolic faith and practice, and therefore as integral to the fullness and unity of the Body of Christ.

4. We confess as proved by most certain warrants of Holy Scripture the historic faith of the undivided church as declared in the three Catholic Creeds: the Apostles', the Nicene, and the Athanasian.

5. Concerning the seven Councils of the undivided Church, we affirm the teaching of the first four Councils and the Christological clarifications of the fifth, sixth, and seventh councils, in so far as they are agreeable

to the Holy Scriptures.

6. We receive The Book of Common Prayer as set forth by the Church of England in 1662, together with the Ordinal attached to the same, as a standard for Anglican doctrine and discipline, and, with the Books which preceded it, as the standard for the Anglican tradition of worship.

7. We receive the Thirty-Nine Articles of Religion of 1571 as expressing fundamental principles of authentic Anglican belief.

Here's a simple acrostic device utilizing the word BEACON that you may find useful for recalling Anglicanism's Core Values:

B   **Bible**–The supremacy of Holy Scripture.

E   **Episcopate**–The Godly historic episcopate.

A   **Articles of Religion**–Fundamental principles of Anglican belief.

C   **Creeds**–The Apostles' Creed, Nicene Creed, and Athanasian Creed

O   **Only** two Sacraments were instituted by Jesus: Baptism and Communion.

N   The BCP is **Nothing** more than the Bible organized for worship.[16]

What About Anglican Theology?

Theology is defined as *a distinctive body of theological opinion*; that is, to have or subscribe to a theology means to follow a particular school of thought or belief system about God and religious issues. Using that definition, it is clear that the Anglican Church does not have a theology that is peculiar to it. We can see from the Lutheran Church, which is based upon the theology of Martin Luther, or the Presbyterian Church, based on the theology of John Calvin, that their theology is based upon the writings of these individuals and, of course, is based upon Scripture.

In the year 1054, a split or schism occurred in the medieval Catholic Church. It divided into the East, which included Jerusalem and Alexandria, and the West, based in Rome. The split led to the development of the modern Roman Catholic and Eastern Orthodox churches. From the time of the schism on, the Roman Catholic Church began to modify the theology that had existed for the first millennia of the Catholic Church in order to meet the perceived needs of their church. Indeed, theologians have developed or modified Christian theologies over the years. Not all changes are bad, but often they depart from the original teachings of Christ. Anglicans, instead, look to the plain meaning of the words of Holy Scripture and teachings of the early church for theological understanding.

> Anglicans look to the plain meaning of the words of Holy Scripture and teachings of the early church for theological understanding.

The position of the Anglican Church toward having a theology was perhaps best expressed by Bishop Thomas Ken's writing in the early 18th century.

> I die in the Holy, Catholic, and Apostolic Faith, professed by the whole Church before the disunion of East and West.[17]

In this case Bishop Ken is stating his belief in the church based upon what the Church has always believed, at all times, and in all places, during the first few hundred years of Christianity. It is an apt statement that Anglicanism is a container for apostolic faith and practice, to be passed along from generation to generation.

One of the most valuable outcomes of the English reformation is the 1662 Book of Common Prayer (BCP), which is still the standard in most of the Anglican world. A great many other churches have borrowed from the BCP, the Lutherans, Methodists, and Presbyterians among them. Even the modern Roman Catholic Mass in English drew from Thomas Cranmer's translations of the early prayers of the Church.

To this day, the BCP and its newer versions suffice to set forth the Anglican strand of the Christian faith. If you take the time to familiarize yourself with the BCP you will find Holy Scripture (usually quoted directly, sometimes paraphrased) along with collects and prayers translated by Cranmer from the early church or composed by him based upon Scripture.

The Bible-based Anglican Book of Common Prayer, in its several version, contains the standard of its apostolic faith and practice. We will learn more about the BCP later.

What do Anglicans Teach?

Let's have a quick look at Thomas Cranmer and Richard Hooker's work as well as Cranmer's *Thirty-Nine Articles of Religion*. Bear in mind that the meaning of *doctrine* is *a body of teachings*, for that's what Hooker and Cranmer were all about in their day. Their teaching wasn't their own. They sought to collect and set forth the historic teaching of the Apostles.

Thomas Cranmer

Thomas Cranmer (1489-1556), Archbishop of Canterbury for King Henry VIII, was a very learned man with perhaps the greatest library in

the realm. Before naming him as Archbishop, King Henry VIII had sent him to Germany as an ambassador, where Cranmer encountered Protestant reformers. From them, Cranmer received an enlightenment concerning the doctrine of salvation that he later gradually introduced into the Anglican Church. The Roman Catholic Church of the day adhered to its medieval theology of meriting salvation via shame, guilt, and works of repentance. The Protestants, on the other hand, who looked only to the plain meaning of the words of Holy Scripture, taught that salvation was the unmerited gift that one receives through faith in Jesus Christ alone. Cranmer agreed with them that it is not because of acts of repentance or by proving oneself worthy that God forgives sinners; rather, it is solely because of Jesus' work on the Cross. It is only one's gratitude for God's unconditional love that can ever lead one's heart to actually loving God more than oneself.

We are greatly blessed by Thomas Cranmer's doctrine of the grateful heart, and by the numerous references to the heart in the Book of Common Prayer. For example, "Unto whom all hearts are open"..."Cleanse the thoughts of our hearts"..."Lift up your hearts"..."Who is able to keep your heart in the knowledge and love of God"..."Feed on Him in your hearts."

Why so much about the heart? Because Jesus, as the Gospels document in His earthly ministry, was most often dealing with the condition of the human heart.

Richard Hooker

Richard Hooker (1554-1600) was an influential Anglican theologian. (Remember, Anglicans have *theologians*—academics who study after the things of God—but Anglicans do not have a *theology* in the sense of their own particular form, system, or branch of Christian thought.) Hooker, with Thomas Cranmer and Matthew Parker,[18] are regarded as cofounders of Anglican doctrine, which is the body of teachings that comprise Anglicanism. Hooker's eight-volume work *Of the Laws of Ecclesiastical Polity* is the classic writing that defines and defends almost every aspect of Anglican religious theory and practice. That doesn't mean that Hooker set forth a theology, only that he was a theologian who carefully studied after and commented on the things of God.

Hooker argued that all positive laws of the church and state are developed from scriptural revelation, ancient tradition, and reason. Today, we often hear of Scripture, tradition, and reason forming a tripod that helps define our Church. What Hooker actually suggested is a hierarchy of authority for the three terms, with Scripture as foundational, then reason and tradition (in that order) as very important but subservient to Scripture. You might think of it as a tricycle with its large front wheel powering and steering and the two little wheels that follow lending balance.

The Thirty-Nine Articles of Religion

The *Thirty-Nine Articles of Religion* are a doctrinal statement developed and written by Archbishop Thomas Cranmer, along with other clergy, in the mid-16th century and approved by Queen Elizabeth I in 1571. The *Thirty-Nine Articles of Religion* helped to define Anglicanism, along with the first four Councils of the Church, the Creeds, and the 1662 Book of Common Prayer.[19] The authority of the Thirty-Nine Articles comes as a result of their agreement with the teaching of Scripture.[20] They were intended to guard against false doctrine creeping into the Church as a result of various matters in dispute at the time, rather than to comprise a comprehensive statement of the faith.

The Thirty-Nine Articles can be grouped for better understanding and ease of use as follows:

- The Substance of Faith (Articles I-V)
- The Rule of Faith (Articles VI-VIII)
- The Life of Faith, or Personal Religion (Article IX-XVIII)
- The Corporate Religion (Articles XIX-XXXIX)

The Thirty-Nine Articles of Religion can be found in the 1928 BCP on page 603 and in the 1979 BCP on page 867. They are a great resource for better understanding the Anglican Church.

The Distinctives of Anglican Worship

The unique characteristics or *distinctives* of Anglican worship originated principally from the writings of Thomas Cranmer, who aimed to create church services where the people and the clergy would participate together in worshiping God.

Before Cranmer, the practice had been for the priest to "perform," with the role of the people limited to being present in church to adore the consecrated elements as they watched the priest serve himself (but not them) communion. Cranmer took seriously the term *liturgy,* from the Greek word *leitourgia,* which means *work* plus *people,* or *the work of the people.* For Cranmer, that meant *all* of God's people, whether ordained or not, working in unison, worshiping Him. Cranmer also wanted Church services to utilize a common liturgy throughout the realm (at that time, church rites varied widely from place to place) and to be spoken in English rather than Latin. He was careful to take the prayers, collects (the ones he wrote himself), and other service elements directly from the Bible, and he either quoted it exactly or closely paraphrased Holy Scripture. Because many of his priests were semiliterate and hardly any of the people had been taught what it meant to be a Christian, he authored the *First Book of Homilies* (1547), which contained twelve sermons mandated by royal decree to be given throughout the realm every Sunday, each to be repeated four times a year. These covered almost everything a Christian needed to know about being a Christian. Later, a *Second Book of Homilies* was added.

Cranmer's 1549 Book of Common Prayer (and his later 1552 BCP) included Morning Prayer, Evening Prayer, the Litany, and Holy Communion, and included the other occasional services for baptism, confirmation, marriage, prayers to be said with the sick, and a funeral service. It contained the Epistle and Gospel readings for the Sunday communion service, along with Old and New Testament readings for daily prayer, as well as canticles and the Psalms. The 1662 edition has remained the official prayer book of the Church of England and many Anglican churches worldwide and appears in over 150 languages.

The Eucharist

The centerpiece of the Anglican worship service is the Eucharist or Holy Communion. Anglicans focus their worship on communion because the sacrament of the Lord's Supper was instituted, indeed commanded, by Christ Himself for the continual remembrance of His life, death, and resurrection, and of the promise that He will come again. In the Eucharist, Christ unites us to His offering of Himself for the forgiveness of sins once and for all. We make real the forgiveness of our sins and the strengthening of our union with Christ and with one another, and we experience a foretaste of the heavenly banquet awaiting us in eternal life.

Three Styles of Worship

The three streams or styles of Anglican worship are Anglo-Catholic, Evangelical, and Charismatic. Although each stream is different in its focus, they do form a single river of praise to our God. All styles emphasize the importance of prayer for the world, for the church, and for individuals. Let's take a look at how the three strands are defined.

> The three streams or styles of Anglican worship are Anglo-Catholic, Evangelical, and Charismatic.

The **Anglo-Catholic** tradition is the most formal. It has been characterized by some as a form of Catholicism without Vatican control, or a form of Protestantism with more elaborate ritual, or, as others would indicate, a great blend of the two.

Fr. Larry Bausch, Rector of Holy Trinity Parish in San Diego, California, defines the Anglo-Catholic tradition as having two essential components. First, it centers on the fully catholic heritage and identity of the Church, continuous with the faith and practice of the undivided Church of the first millennium. It emphasizes the historic essence of the Scriptures, creeds, sacraments, and ministry. Second, Anglo-Catholic worship is typically formal while fully participatory, and often uses elaborate traditional vestments, candles, incense, Sanctus bells, and chanting. This style of worship is frequently referred to as "High Church" due to its formal nature that captures the beauty of the rituals.

The **Evangelical** tradition emphasizes the significance of the Protestant aspects of Anglicanism's identity. It stresses the importance of the authority of Scripture, preaching, justification by faith, and one's own personal conversion. Evangelical Anglicanism is rooted in Thomas Cranmer's introduction into the Church of England of Martin Luther's justification by faith based on the plain meaning of the words of Scripture. It replaced the medieval church's theology of salvation through shame, guilt, and works of repentance. It is the emphasis on evangelistic fervor that spread Anglicanism around the globe, making it the third largest Christian body today. Evangelical Anglican church services tend to minimize vestments and other visible worship symbols and to emphasize evangelistic preaching.

Charismatic worship takes place in a more relaxed environment, yet the traditional elements of a Book of Common Prayer service remain. A "charismatic movement" occurred in mainline Christian denominations in the second half of the 20th century, one that included the Roman Catholic, Lutheran, and Episcopal Churches. The Charismatic movement was founded on the belief that Christians may be "filled with" or "baptized in" the Holy Spirit as an experience following salvation and accompanied by manifestations of the Holy Spirit. Charismatic (*charisma*, Greek for *gift or favor given*) describes the understanding that the gifts of the Holy Spirit encountered in the New Testament (e.g., 1 Corinthians 12-14) are definitely available to believers today. These include signs and wonders, speaking in tongues, interpretation of tongues, prophecy, healing, and discernment of spirits. Anglican charismatic services are characterized by contemporary worship music, openness to manifestations of the Holy Spirit, and a pervading informality, though Sunday services are nonetheless centered in the Eucharist, as is any Anglican Eucharistic service.

You may hear the three styles referred to simply as Traditional, Contemporary, and Charismatic. The Contemporary format is often used with the Evangelical strand of worship. Many ACNA churches offer two and some offer all three services.[21] You select from these depending on how the Lord leads you. Some people will attend more than one Sunday service or alternate attendance among them.[22]

Which service do I prefer? Well, let's just say it's the one I'm in at the time! Why? None of the three worship styles reject the others; they simply shift the focus from here to there, downplaying this to emphasize that.

It bears repeating: None of the three worship styles actually reject the others; they simply shift the focus from here to there, downplaying one aspect to emphasize another.

Session Three
Questions for Preparation
and Discussion

Questions for Preparation

1. Why was it important for ACNA to adopt a set of core beliefs?

2. True or false: Anglican theology was developed based on the writings of Luther and Calvin. Explain your answer.

3. Hooker was an influential Anglican theologian. Some refer to his positive laws of the church as being like a tricycle. What do the three wheels of the tricycle represent in that model? According to Hooker, how are the positive laws of the Church and State developed?

4. The Creed of St. Athanasius is a great resource. What does it say about Jesus Christ?

Questions for Discussion

1. Which stream or style of Anglican worship (Anglo-Catholic, Evangelical, or Charismatic) do you enjoy the most or feel most comfortable with? Why?

2. Do you think that over time your preferences might change? Explain.

3. Bishop Thomas Ken, writing in the 18th century, famously said, "There is no Anglican theology. That is to say, Anglicanism does not intend to teach any doctrine that is peculiar to it." How do you interpret that statement?

Session Four

The Liturgy and More

Anglicans do some things during a church service that newcomers might not understand. Issues as simple as what books to use and when to kneel, sit, or stand can be confusing at first. For visitors to feel comfortable and to be able to participate in the worship service, we need to explain our liturgy in very simple terms.

What is Corporate Worship?

In *corporate worship*, we come together and unite ourselves with other believers to acknowledge the holiness of God, to hear God's Word, to offer prayers, to listen to God, and to celebrate the sacrament of the Eucharist. Remember Jesus' promise about corporate worship and prayer:

Where two or three are gathered in my name, there am I with them. (Matthew 18:20)

As the congregation focuses on praise and worship of our Lord and Savior corporately, the individual's spiritual awareness of God's presence is heightened as well. In worshipping together we are spiritually prepared and motivated, as a congregation, to go into the world as faithful Christians and face the realities of life.

Corporate worship is so very biblical. David, a man after God's own heart, wrote:

I rejoice with those who said to me, "Let us go to the house of the Lord." (Psalm 122:1)

Glorify the Lord with me, and let us exalt his name together. (Psalm 34:3)

We are to exalt God in our corporate worship and, according to Scripture, God loves it. "He inhabits the praises of his people" (Psalm 22:3).

> To be a lone Christian is to be a dead Christian.

Michael Nazir-Ali puts the need for corporate worship in very simple terms. "First of all, it must be possible for God's people to gather. To be a lone Christian is to be a dead Christian. We must gather together to hear God's Word, to celebrate the sacraments, to learn from one another, and to pray for one another."[23]

Personal Reflection

Bishop Nazir-Ali states that "To be a lone Christian is to be a dead Christian." What is your understanding of this statement?

The purpose of the Book of Common Prayer was, and is, to encourage, facilitate, and regularize corporate worship, according to the biblical model and authority. (Of course, the BCP can and should be used for private devotions too. I hope you have a copy in your home. You can find several sources for it on the Internet.) It was propagated because Thomas Cranmer saw that not only was there no rhyme or reason to the varying liturgical rites in different parts of the realm (that is, they had little in common, so that a visitor couldn't relate to the service), but also because the congregation was, for all practical purposes, excluded from the worship conducted by the priests.[24] You can think of the Book of Common Prayer as a manual to facilitate corporate worship when two or three are gathered together in His name.

Archbishop Robert Duncan of the Anglican Church in North America defines the Book of Common Prayer perfectly. "The Book of Common Prayer is nothing more than the Bible organized for worship."[25]

A typical Sunday service in the Anglican Church is a Eucharist or the Lord's Supper. The service is in two parts. The *first* part is the Word of God, which includes readings from the Old Testament, New Testament (Epistle), and a reading from one of the Gospels. We listen to a sermon relating to the readings. We say the Nicene Creed, the Prayers of the People, and a confession of sin to prepare us for Holy Communion, and end with the passing God's peace to one another. The *second* part is the celebration of Holy Communion or the Lord's Supper. This is a time when we receive the elements (bread and wine) and commune with the Lord, by faith, in our own personal way. When the Communion is completed the priest gives a blessing, followed by a recessional hymn, and the service ends with a dismissal. It is a very powerful and uplifting service that renews us to serve the Lord with all our heart, mind, and spirit.

The 1979 BCP Holy Eucharist Rite I is the more traditional service, while Holy Eucharist Rite II is more contemporary and often used with the Evangelical strand of worship. Both Rite I and Rite II are easy to follow in the Book of Common Prayer.

Why Is Baptism Important?

Baptism is one of the two sacraments instituted by Christ himself; the other is Holy Communion. Baptism is the sacrament by which God adopts us as his children and makes us members of Christ's body—which is the Church—and inheritors of the kingdom of God. All four of the Gospels tell us that John the Baptist baptized Jesus in the River Jordan. After Jesus emerged from the water, the Holy Spirit descended upon Him, in the form of a dove. The voice of God spoke from heaven, declaring Jesus to be "My well-beloved son." That's why those desiring to become Christians are baptized with water in the name of the Father, and of the Son, and of the Holy Spirit.

> The voice of God spoke from heaven, declaring Jesus to be "My well-beloved son."

According to Matthew's gospel, Jesus in His post-resurrection appearance to his disciples in Galilee commanded them to baptize:

> Go therefore and make disciples of all nations, baptizing them in the name of the Father and of the Son and of the Holy Spirit. (Matthew 28:19)

Consequently, only baptized Christians are eligible to receive communion in an Anglican Church, as they are considered one of Christ's own. In the Anglican Church in North America, every layperson is expected to present their children, and those they have led to the Lord, for Baptism and Confirmation.[26]

Why Do Anglicans Baptize Infants?

The Anglican Church baptizes infants and children who are not able to answer for themselves, doing so on the basis of the faith and repentance of their parents and godparents and on the commitment of the parents and grandparents that the children will be brought up as Christians in the fellowship of the Church. Article 27 of the Articles of Religion defines Baptism for the Anglican Church and makes a clear statement about Baptism of youth:

> Baptism is not only a sign of profession, and mark of difference, whereby Christian men are discerned from others that be not christened, but it is also a sign of Regeneration or New-Birth, whereby, as by an instrument, they that receive Baptism rightly are grafted into the Church; the promises of the forgiveness of sin, and of our adoption to be the sons of God by the Holy Ghost, are visibly signed and sealed, Faith is confirmed, and Grace increased by virtue of prayer unto God.

> The Baptism of young children is in any wise to be retained in the Church, as most agreeable with the institution of Christ.

In Canon Chuck Collins' book *Cranmer's Church*, he cites several good additional reasons[27] why infants are baptized, including, "Infants are baptized because there is no reason to withhold from them the greatest gift of all, welcoming them into the community of believers who will love them and bring them into a relationship with Jesus."

From a parent's perspective it is very exciting to have an infant son or daughter baptized. I vividly recall when water was being poured over our children's heads in the name of the Father, and of the Son, and of the Holy Spirit. It was an emotional moment knowing that they were the newest members of God's Kingdom. I am happy to say the same thing happened as I watched my grandchildren being baptized. What a beautiful and visible sign of God's amazing grace in action!

What Is Confirmation? How Important Is It?

The 1979 BCP (page 412) defines Anglican Confirmation this way:

> In the course of their Christian development, those baptized at an early age are expected, when they are ready and have been duly prepared, to make a mature public affirmation of their faith and commitment to the responsibilities of their Baptism and to receive the laying on of hands by the Bishop.

For Anglicans, Confirmation is a pivotal event in their spiritual formation. It is the occasion to publicly ratify one's vows made in Baptism, and can be especially meaningful to those who were baptized before the age of reason when Baptismal vows were made on their behalf by their parents and others.

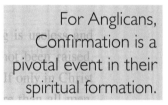

For Anglicans, Confirmation is a pivotal event in their spiritual formation.

The Bishop, by his apostolic authority, lays hands on those to be confirmed (1) that they may be strengthened with the Holy Spirit, (2) that they may increase in the knowledge and obedience of God's Word, and (3) that they may be preserved unto eternal life.

Although Confirmation is not a salvation issue, it has important spiritual benefits, including:

Confession Publicly acknowledging Christ is transformative, as seen in Jesus' statement, "So everyone who acknowledges me before men, I also will acknowledge before my Father who is in heaven" (Matthew 10:32) and in Joshua's confession "But as for me and my house, we will serve the Lord" (Joshua 24:15).

Accountability Publicly accepting the responsibility for our own spiritual formation sets us firmly on the path to increasing maturity in our Christian walk.

Offering In Confirmation, we show forth God's praise not only with our lips, but also by giving ourselves up into His service. (See Romans 12:1 and the General Thanksgiving in the 1979 BCP, page 101.)

Commissioning In the laying on of hands and in prayer, the Bishop commissions the candidates in the power of the Holy Spirit for the service to which the Lord has called them. (See Ephesians 2:10.)

Be sure to ask your rector if you have any questions about the importance of Confirmation in your life or in the lives of those you love.

What is Eucharistic Discipline?

Eucharistic discipline is the term applied to the regulations and practices associated with a person's preparation for partaking of the Eucharist. Different Christian traditions require varying degrees of preparation, which may include fasting, prayer, confession, and repentance. There's a reason for this, as Paul warns in 1 Corinthians 11:29: "For those who eat and drink without discerning the body of Christ eat and drink judgment on themselves." See also Article XXV of the Articles of Religion where Paul's warning is repeated and we are admonished to worthily receive Communion: "And in such [persons] only as worthily receive the same they [the sacraments] have a wholesome effect or operation."

For Anglicans, the preparation is set forth in the Eucharistic service: prayer, confession of sin, the peace (being in love and charity with all persons), affirmation of our faith, lifting up our hearts unto the Lord, thanksgiving, praise, and presenting to the Lord ourselves, our souls and bodies, to be a reasonable, holy, and living sacrifice unto the Lord. So what is required of us to take communion? The 1979 BCP (page 860) puts it this way: "That we should examine our lives, repent of our sins, and be in love and charity with all people." The proper attitude is summed up in these words, often said just before receiving communion: "We do not presume to come to this Thy table, O merciful Lord, trusting in our own righteousness, but in thy manifold and great mercies" (1928 BCP, 82; 1979 BCP, 337).

The Anglican Church uses bread (wafers, usually) and wine for

Holy Communion. The terms "Eucharist" and "Communion" are used somewhat interchangeably, although it may be helpful to think of the Eucharist as the sacramental rite itself and Communion as your participation in it. Even though fermented wine is called for, you will find that consecrated grape juice is also available in some churches. The consecrated elements are always offered together. Only a bishop or a priest may be the celebrant at the Eucharist, but at least one other person must be present. Matthew makes this point perfectly clear as he writes the words of Jesus:

> For where two or three come together in my name, there I am with them. (Matthew 18:20)

Session Four
Questions for Preparation
and Discussion

Questions for Preparation

1. What does Article XXV of the Articles of Religion (1928 BCP, page 603; 1979 BCP, page 867) say about the number of sacraments ordained of Christ? What do they accomplish, and how they are to be utilized?

2. Why must a person be baptized in order to receive Holy Communion in the Anglican Church?

   Note: If for some reason you have not been baptized or if you are not sure if you have been, please check with your rector or pastor to resolve the issue.

3. Why does the Anglican Church baptize infants?

4. Article XXV also lists five additional sacraments supported by scripture. List the five sacraments and explain the purpose of each.

Questions for Discussion

1. If someone says something to the effect that they're a believer but don't feel the need to attend church, how would you respond?

2. Do you remember what was special or memorable about your own baptism? If you were not baptized, would you share the reason?

3. What was Jesus' position concerning baptism? Why?

4. What is the purpose of Confirmation?

Session Five

The Role of the Laity

As I thought about the idea of *Celebrating Anglicanism,* I wondered how the Anglican Church defines the role of laypersons. I was referred to the Constitution and Canons of the Anglican Church in North America (ACNA) for the answer. I must admit I had never read the Constitution or the Canons of any church prior to this time, so I wasn't sure what to expect. I understand the need for a constitution and what it does for an organization, but what about *canons*? Well, canons are sort of like rules and regulations that are needed to implement a church constitution. It was a breath of fresh air for me to learn that ACNA's canons are quite minimalist in their approach, and that they employ the principle of *subsidiarity*, i.e., they leave decision making at the local level for all matters and details that can wisely be decided at that level. That means only those matters that really need to be dealt with at the top level of authority are covered in ACNA's Canons.

It says something crucially important about ACNA that the Canons actually spell out the role of the laity in the Church: Laypersons in the Anglican Church in North America occupy a position of robust equal partnership with the ordained clergy.

> Laypersons in the Anglican Church in North America occupy a position of robust equal partnership with the ordained clergy.

That's fine, but what about specifics? What do the Canons have to say about the actual duties of the laity? The answer is worth sharing here in its entirety.

Canon 10

Of the Laity

Section 1 - Concerning Ministry

The people of God are the chief agents of the mission of the Church to extend the Kingdom of God by so presenting Jesus Christ in the power of the Holy Spirit that people will come to put their trust in God through Him, know Him as Savior, and serve Him as Lord in the fellowship of the Church. The effective ministry of the Church is the responsibility of the laity no less than it is the responsibility of the bishop, priests, and deacons.

Canon 10 goes on to define duties for the laity.

Section 2 – Concerning Duties of the Laity

It shall be the duty of every member of this Church:

1. **To worship God, the Father, and the Son and the Holy Spirit**, every Lord's Day in a Church unless reasonably prevented;

2. **To engage regularly in the reading and study of Holy Scripture and the Doctrine of the Church** as found in Article I of the Constitution of this Church;

3. **To observe their baptismal vows**, to lead an upright and sober life, and not give scandal to the Church;

4. **To present their children and those they have led to the Lord for baptism and confirmation;**

5. **To give regular financial support** to the Church, with the biblical tithe as the minimum standard of giving;

6. **To practice forgiveness daily** according to our Lord's teaching;

7. **To receive worthily the Sacrament of Holy Communion** as often as reasonable;

8. **To observe the feasts and fasts** of the Church set forth in the Anglican formularies;

9. **To continue his or her instruction in the Faith** so as to remain an effective minister for the Lord Jesus Christ;

10. **To devote themselves to the ministry of Christ among those who do**

not know Him, utilizing the gifts that the Holy Spirit gives them, for the effective extension of Christ's Kingdom.

Personal Reflection

ACNA Canon 10 indicates that lay members of the church are to be effective ministers for the Lord Jesus Christ. How effective are you as a minister for Christ? In what ways might you become a more effective minister for Christ?

I was surprised how much I learned about the duties of the laity from reading Canon 10. In fact, I found it so interesting that I went on to read all the Canons. I highly recommend at least reviewing them, if not reading them all the way through. The ACNA Constitution can be found in Appendix D. The Constitution and Canons are both available on the ACNA web site at *anglicanchurch.net.*

Canon 10, Section 1, "Concerning Ministry," reads in part, "It is incumbent for every lay member of the Church to become an effective minister of the gospel of Jesus Christ, one who is spiritually qualified, **gifted**, called, and mature in the faith." (Emphasis added)

And Section 2, "Concerning the Duties of the Laity," reads in part " … utilizing the **gifts** that the Holy Spirit gives them."

The Holy Spirit is mentioned in both sections, which indicates we need to have a better understanding of what is being referred to in each case. What are the gifts of the Holy Spirit that we should be utilizing in our ministries as laity?

The Apostle Paul describes spiritual gifts in his letters to the churches in Rome, Corinth, and Ephesus. The list below is not all-inclusive, but covers most of what we may see from time to time in our churches.

Word of Wisdom	Word of Knowledge
Faith	Gift of Healing
Working of miracles	Discernment

Speaking in tongues	Interpretation of tongues
Service	Administration
Teaching	Prophesy
Apostleship	Shepherd or pastor
Evangelism	

Keep in mind that spiritual gifts are given by the Holy Spirit only as needed and only by Him. The same person may receive different gifts at different times. (Someone may ask, "What is the most important gift?" That's easy: It's the one you need at the time!)

Paul writes:

All these are empowered by one and the same Spirit, who apportions to each one individually as he wills. (1 Corinthians 12:11 ESV)

A person may have more than one spiritual gift depending on his or her needs. The key is to be ready to receive the gift and use it to do the Lord's work.

In summary, then, laypersons and the ordained clergy share equally the *governance* and the *ministry* of ACNA. Representation in the councils of the Church is equal, and all representatives vote as brothers and sisters, not as separate "houses." "The chief agents of this mission to extend the Kingdom of God are the people of God," meaning all of the clergy and all of the laypersons together (ACNA Constitution, Article III.1).

Each lay member of the church must accept the responsibility stated in the Canons to become and remain "an effective minister for the Lord Jesus Christ." You should realize by now that you *already are*, in fact, a minister. The only question is whether you are becoming an effective one!

Session Five
Questions for Preparation
and Discussion

Session Five

Questions for Preparation

1. ACNA Canon 10, Section 2, lists ten duties of lay members of the Church.

    a. In which of these duties do you see yourself needing some improvement?

    b. What could you do to improve the areas you identified?

Questions for Discussion

1. In what areas might you see yourself as being gifted spiritually?
2. What leads you to that conclusion?
3. How are you using your spiritual gifts with the church?

Session Six

Happenings Beyond the Local Parish

We defined the term *Anglican* in Week Two, but what about the term *Anglican Communion? Communion* is defined as a group of Christians with a common religious faith who practice the same rites so as to be in "communion" with one another. So, then, what is the Anglican Communion?

The Anglican Communion

The Anglican Communion is the worldwide fellowship of Anglican provinces based on their historic relationship with the Church of England and acknowledged commonality of Christian faith as expressed in the 1662 Book of Common Prayer, the Thirty-Nine Articles of Religion, and by adherence to Anglican practices. When England became a colonial power, everywhere the Empire went the Church of England was sure to follow. Sometimes the Empire resisted; mostly it cooperated. The Church of England spread beyond the Empire to Asia, Africa, and South America.

Founded in London in 1799, the Church Missionary Society attracted thousands of men and women to serve as missionaries. Instead of propagating "branch offices" they raised up indigenous leaders among the different peoples they encountered, who then adapted Anglicanism to their own cultures. Today there are 38 major Anglican Provinces globally, not counting ACNA. Our province, ACNA, is recognized by archbishops who represent about 80 percent of all Anglicans, but it has yet to be received into the Anglican Communion. The difficulty still to be resolved is the existing membership of the Episcopal Church in the Anglican Communion; at this writing, 22 of the provinces have declared themselves to be in either impaired or broken relationship with The Episcopal Church (TEC).

The Anglican Communion is also an international association of national and regional Anglican churches, as there is no single "Anglican Church" with universal authority. Each national or regional church has full autonomy. As the name suggests, the Anglican Communion is an association of churches that are in full communion with the Church of England (which may be regarded as the "mother church" of the worldwide communion). The principal primate—the leader of a church within the Anglican Communion who usually holds the title and office of Archbishop—is the Archbishop of Canterbury, who is considered a "first among equals." The status of full communion means, ideally, that there is mutual agreement on essential doctrines, and that full participation in the sacramental life of each national church is available to all of the others.

The worldwide Anglican Communion spans 164 countries and has 80 million members. Remember, we Anglicans are the third largest Christian group internationally, behind the Roman Catholic and Eastern Orthodox Churches. Growth is taking place at a rapid pace among the Anglican churches of the Global South (countries located in the Southern Hemisphere).

The Anglican Church in North America

The birth of our new province in North America—ACNA—is both historic and exciting. At this writing the Anglican Church in North America unites more than 100,000 Anglicans in about 1,000 parishes within some 30 dioceses in the United States and Canada.

When many Episcopal Churches, or groups of parishioners, and individual clergy decided to disaffiliate from the Episcopal Church over theological differences, they needed the episcopal oversight of a bishop and some sort of a spiritual home base. Provinces in the Global South— Uganda, Argentina, Bolivia, Brazil, Kenya, Rwanda and Nigeria—each offered temporary "spiritual homes." In the interim between my parish's disaffiliation from the Episcopal Church in 2004 and the formation of ACNA in 2009, we had to find an Anglican home for episcopal oversight. What a debt of gratitude we owe Bishop Evans Kisekka, Diocese of Luwero, Uganda, for his very kindly and gracious oversight during those difficult years! At the same time, Archbishop Henry Orombi, Primate of the Anglican Church of Uganda, gave us his untiring encouragement. Both of these godly men made numerous trips to California to support us, pray for us, and encourage us during that five-year period. In the years since those days, the bond of fellowship between us has deepened, and there have been numerous trips by our clergy and laity, and by theirs also, between Uganda and California.

Being under the spiritual authority of provinces in the Global South gave the disaffiliated orthodox parishes time to organize a province-in-formation that would become ACNA. It also allowed clergy to remain as clergy in the Anglican Communion and to continue their ministry as such.

As an outstanding benefit of these close relationships with the Global South, several bishops and archbishops came to the United States to share not only their insights on the importance of maintaining historical core values as Anglicans, but also their own amazing stories of church growth and ministries.

ACNA is in the mainstream of Christianity, both globally and historically. It is biblically faithful in following Jesus as a part of the one holy, catholic and apostolic church. More information about ACNA may be found at **www.anglicanchurch.net**.

Birthing an ACNA Diocese

My own diocese within ACNA is the Diocese of Western Anglicans. Its short history is pretty informative of larger issues, so I'll recap it briefly.

In 2007, my parish had been disaffiliated from the Episcopal Church and under Ugandan episcopal oversight for almost three years. We were prayerfully awaiting developments that would lead to an orthodox Anglican structure in America when lightning flashed ominously that February. The Primates of the Anglican Communion, meeting in Dar es Salaam, Tanzania, resolved *unanimously* that churches that had disaffiliated from the Episcopal Church *must return to it* under an arrangement where the Episcopal Church promised "orthodox" oversight by means of a special bishop appointed for the former Episcopal parishes. The so-called "Primatial Vicar" would, of course, be under the oversight of the Episcopal Church. This was definitely not an acceptable arrangement for oversight for those who had disaffiliated from the Episcopal Church, and it demanded emergency action on two fronts: Educating the primates of the Anglican Communion about the magnitude of the apostasy (rejecting Biblical truth) in the Episcopal Church, and demonstrating to them that an independent orthodox Anglican structure was possible in America.

Only sixty days later, lay and clergy delegates from 14 orthodox Anglican congregations in Southern California and Arizona met to begin the process of forming a new "diocese-in-waiting." The founding congregations had disassociated from the Episcopal Church in the United States and placed themselves under Anglican bishops in Argentina, Bolivia, Kenya, Rwanda, and Uganda, all provinces of the worldwide Anglican Communion. These supportive Anglican Communion primates were watching to see if groups of churches like ours across the country could "get their acts together."

The organizational structure of what would become the new diocese (we called ourselves the "Association of Western Anglican Congregations" at the time) was accomplished in only 120 days. In that short time we became a diocese-in-formation

> Western Anglicans is a minimalist diocesan structure that exists only to serve the congregations in their leading role in ministry.

flourishing in shared ministry and promise for the future. Our bishop and lay president are co-chairpersons of a diocese managed, except in spiritual matters, by equal representation of clergy and laity voting unicamerally (no separate "houses" of clergy and laity). Not only that, Western Anglicans is a minimalist diocesan structure that exists only to serve the congregations in their leading role in ministry. We praise our Lord Jesus Christ for his provision and faithfulness as this project and others like it unfolded across the United States and Canada, helping to make the Anglican Church in North America a reality. We eventually had the joy of being the first diocese accepted into ACNA! That may have been just a coincidence, but it was pretty special to head the list the day the initial ACNA dioceses were proclaimed. The consecration of our first diocesan bishop was a joyous event and celebration.[28]

The creation of ACNA itself is another God-directed story. Suffice it to say that the sacrificial hard work of ACNA's predecessor, Common Cause Partnership and its lead bishops, with God's help, is what made this magnificent achievement possible.

What is GAFCON?

Over 1,000 senior lay and clergy leaders and 300 bishops and their wives, from seventeen provinces in the Anglican Communion representing 35 million church-going Anglicans, attended the Global Anglican Future Conference (GAFCON) in Jerusalem in June of 2008. GAFCON was truly a gathering of representatives of orthodox Anglicans from all corners of the globe.

The goals of GAFCON were, and still are, to:

- Provide an opportunity for fellowship as well as to continue to experience and proclaim the transforming love of Christ.
- Develop a renewed understanding of our identity as Anglican Christians.
- Prepare for an Anglican future in which the Gospel is uncompromised and Christ-centered mission is a top priority.

The Global Anglican Future Conference met in plenary and small group sessions for an entire week and then issued the GAFCON statement. The statement contained the *Jerusalem Declaration*, which is the foundational document of the global Fellowship of Confessing Anglicans (FCA) movement initiated at GAFCON. FCA includes provinces, dioceses, churches, missionary jurisdictions, and church organizations, as well as individual members. The goal of FCA is to reform, heal, and revitalize the Anglican Communion and to expand its mission to the world. FCA is united and committed to working and praying together in the common mission of Christ. It is a "confessing fellowship" in that its members confess the faith of Christ crucified, stand firm for the gospel in the global and Anglican context, and affirm a contemporary rule, the *Jerusalem Declaration*, to guide Anglicanism for the future. You can join the Fellowship of Confessing Anglicans yourself at *www.fca.net*.

The Jerusalem Declaration: Where We Stand

The *Jerusalem Declaration* is a clear, orthodox statement for Anglicans everywhere to follow as a means of keeping the faith once for all delivered to the saints. It is the most important contemporary statement of what it means to be an Anglican today and for the future. Every Anglican should have a basic understanding of what the document states

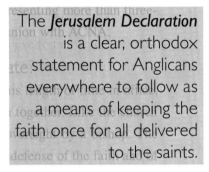

The *Jerusalem Declaration* is a clear, orthodox statement for Anglicans everywhere to follow as a means of keeping the faith once for all delivered to the saints.

about Anglicanism today. Read each tenet of the *Jerusalem Declaration* carefully. Try to fully absorb what has been written and agreed upon by all who were in attendance at GAFCON in Jerusalem, David's Royal City. As the declaration was being read aloud in plenary session for a final vote of approval, 1,300 people arose in a spontaneous eruption of joy in the Spirit. The reader was unable to continue while the deafening praise rolled like ocean waves throughout the vast room, as people of all cultures danced, strangers hugged, and tears of joy flowed without restraint. Eventually— long, long minutes into the celebration—the Chair simply asked for a vote by acclamation, only to be drowned out once more by more thundering agreement and further celebration. (Yes, the delegates had printed copies so they knew exactly what they were approving.)

There are 14 statements in the *Jerusalem Declaration*. As you read each tenet or statement, ask yourself this question: Do I agree *in my heart* with this statement? If you have an issue or concern with one of the tenets, go to the Bible and look to see what God's word has to say about it. Feel free to share your concern with your small group or to seek guidance from your clergy.

The Jerusalem Declaration

IN THE NAME of God the Father, God the Son, and God the Holy Spirit: We, the participants in the Global Anglican Future Conference, have met in the land of Jesus' birth. We express our loyalty as disciples to the King of kings, the Lord Jesus. We joyfully embrace his command to proclaim the reality of his kingdom, which he first announced in this land. The gospel of the kingdom is the good news of salvation, liberation and transformation for all. In light of the above, we agree to chart a way forward together that promotes and protects the biblical gospel and mission to the world, solemnly declaring the following tenets of orthodoxy which underpin our Anglican identity.

1. We rejoice in the gospel of God through which we have been saved by grace through faith in Jesus Christ by the power of the Holy Spirit. Because God first loved us, we love him and as believers bring forth fruits of love, ongoing repentance, lively hope and thanksgiving to God in all things.

2. We believe the Holy Scriptures of the Old and New Testaments to be the Word of God written and to contain all things necessary for salvation. The Bible is to be translated, read, preached, taught and obeyed in its plain and canonical sense and is respectful of the church's historic and consensual reading.

3. We uphold the four Ecumenical Councils and the three historic reeds as expressing the rule of faith of the one holy, catholic and apostolic Church.

4. We uphold the Thirty-Nine Articles as containing the true doctrine of the Church agreeing with God's Word and as authoritative for Anglicans today.

5. We gladly proclaim and submit to the unique and universal Lordship of Jesus Christ, the Son of God, humanity's only Savior from sin, judgment and hell, who lived the life we could not live and died the death that we deserve. By his atoning death and glorious resurrection, he secured the redemption of all who come to him in repentance and faith.

6. We rejoice in our Anglican sacramental and liturgical heritage as an expression of the gospel, and we uphold the 1662 Book of Common Prayer as a true and authoritative standard of worship and prayer, to be translated and locally adapted for each culture.

7. We recognize that God has called and gifted bishops, priests and

deacons in historic succession to equip all the people of God for their ministry in the world. We uphold the classic Anglican Ordinal as an authoritative standard of clerical orders.

8. We acknowledge God's creation of humankind as male and female and the unchangeable standard of Christian marriage between one man and one woman as the proper place for sexual intimacy and the basis of the family. We repent of our failures to maintain this standard and call for a renewed commitment to lifelong fidelity in marriage and abstinence for those who are not married.

9. We gladly accept the Great Commission of the risen Lord to make disciples of all nations, to seek those who do not know Christ, and to baptize, teach and bring new believers to maturity.

10. We are mindful of our responsibility to be good stewards of God's creation, to uphold and advocate justice in society, and to seek relief and empowerment of the poor and needy.

11. We are committed to the unity of all those who know and love Christ and to building authentic ecumenical relationships. We recognize the orders and jurisdiction of those Anglicans who uphold orthodox faith and practice, and we encourage them to join us in this declaration.

12. We celebrate the God-given diversity among us, which enriches our global fellowship, and we acknowledge freedom in secondary matters. We pledge to work together to seek the mind of Christ on issues that divide us.

13. We reject the authority of those churches and leaders who have denied the orthodox faith in word or deed. We pray for them and call on them to repent and return to the Lord.

14. We rejoice at the prospect of Jesus' coming again in glory, and while we await this final event of history, we praise Him for the way he builds up his church through his Spirit by miraculously changing lives.

The 14 statements are the foundation of our apostolic faith today, and we must not let any of the statements be modified for convenience or any other ungodly reason. We need to review them on occasion and keep the concepts fresh in our minds for our own benefit because the *Jerusalem*

Declaration defines for orthodox Anglicans who we are and what we believe as authentic Christians.

Since Celebrate Anglicanism was published in 2012 GAFCON 2013 was held in Nairobi, Kenya, in October of 2013. Over 1,300 delegates including 331 bishops representing 38 countries were in attendance. The conference was exciting, informative and spiritual with a lot of prayer and praise for our Lord and Savior Jesus Christ.

At the conclusion of the conference a paper was released known as The Nairobi Communiqué. The final part of the Communiqué is The Nairobi Commitment. It has nine parts all of which are powerful statements that all orthodox Anglicans should be familiar with and support.

The Nairobi Commitment can be found in Appendix F.

Personal Reflection

Why do you think the Jerusalem Declaration is important to members of an Anglican Church in North America?

The Oxford Statement

The Oxford Statement challenges provinces, dioceses, and parishes to adopt the *Jerusalem Declaration* as a statement of their beliefs.

In October 2010, the GAFCON leadership met in Oxford, England. They gathered as Bishops in Council and as the elected leaders of many provinces and national churches of the Anglican Communion, collectively representing more than forty million Anglicans. Their purpose was to declare that we were now entering a new era for the Anglican Communion. They issued a paper titled *The Oxford Statement*, which contained an introduction and 14 statements of great importance in strengthening orthodox Anglican churches in the worldwide Anglican Communion. *The Oxford Statement*, which can be found in Appendix E, challenges provinces, dioceses, and parishes to adopt the *Jerusalem Declaration* as a statement of their beliefs. It also invites individuals to reaffirm what we have always believed in Anglicanism, doing so by adopting the *Jerusalem Declaration* themselves as a statement of their own faith and joining in partnership with GAFCON in working to win the world to Christ.

The *Oxford Statement* deserves your careful reading because it states the real character of the global orthodox Anglican Church, including ACNA. What an exciting clear and concise challenge to all Anglicans to stand firm for the orthodox faith passed down through the generations to us! Hallelujah!

Session Six
Questions for Preparation
and Discussion

Questions for Preparation

1. Define the term *Anglican Communion*.
2. Why was it important for Anglicans in North American to create a new province?
3. What was the purpose in forming new dioceses-in-formation (such as the one that evolved into the Diocese of Western Anglicans)?
4. Are there any tenets of the *Jerusalem Declaration* that you are not completely comfortable with? If so, which ones and why not?

Questions for Discussion

1. Which of the three goals of the GAFCON meeting in Jerusalem do you see as most important to the Anglican Church? Explain your answer.
2. Which tenets of the *Jerusalem Declaration* are most important to you? Why?
3. Do you think is it important for ACNA to gain membership in the Anglican Communion? Why or why not?
4. Do you believe that the Anglican Church has a strong and vibrant future? Why or why not?

Session Seven

Becoming a Fisher of Men

Putting it All Together

We have had a long and interesting journey as we have learned about the very beginnings of the Anglican Church all the way to the current status of the worldwide Anglican Communion. We learned about the Anglican Church in North America (ACNA), the new province-in-waiting, and about the formation of my own Diocese of Western Anglicans.

We have learned that the very roots of our Anglican Church were taking hold in England as early as the year AD 43. The Church of England began to take shape as it defined itself based primarily upon Scripture and secondarily on tradition and reason in the 1500s. Thomas Cranmer prepared the first Book of Common Prayer in order to provide form and consistency in our Anglican services and to ensure a Bible-based church. He was responsible for having services in English and developing a liturgy that provided for participation in the service by all members of the congregation. At the bequest of King Henry VIII in 1539, Sir Thomas Cromwell[29] retained Myles Coverdale[30] to publish an authorized version of the Bible for the Church of England. It was authorized for public use and was placed in every church in England so people could read it. It became known as the "Great Bible" and was over 14 inches thick.

We learned that orthodox Anglicans today believe what the orthodox Christian Church has always believed, at all times, and in all places, from the very birth of Christianity. It is the faith that was once for all entrusted to the Saints (Jude 1:3) and handed down from generation to generation. We have the responsibility to defend our orthodox faith from today's secular-progressive world.

Our Responsibility

What are we to do with what we have been given by God Himself? Jesus states it clearly in Matthew's Gospel,

"Go therefore and make disciples of all nations..." (Matthew 28:19 ESV)

As orthodox Anglicans, our role is clearly defined. We are to help shoulder the responsibility for ministry in our churches. We are to continue to learn through discipleship training and by actually becoming ambassadors for Christ in our homes and in the world. Most importantly, we are to utilize the gifts that the Holy Spirit gives us for the effective extension of Christ's Kingdom.

> As orthodox Anglicans, our role is clearly defined. We are to help shoulder the responsibility for ministry in our churches.

Keep in mind that the disciples were with Jesus for three years of training that prepared them to become Apostles. They were in a learning mode as disciples. After receiving the Holy Spirit on Pentecost, they became Apostles and were sent out as teachers to build the Kingdom (Acts 1:8).

We cannot continue to learn about Jesus Christ and grow in faith without actually sharing the good news about Him with others. It is imperative that we, as Christians, move from being in preparation mode or at study to being an effective voice for Christ where we are planted. What we have taken in we now must give out and share with others, especially those who don't know the Lord.

Celebrate Anglicanism

As a result of our seven-week journey we should be equipped and emboldened to share the knowledge we have gained about our Anglican Church. If that is the case, then we are ready to celebrate Anglicanism by sharing our faith and our tradition with others.

As I think about the question "Why do I love the Anglican Church?" I begin to get excited about what Anglicans have to offer to a world in such great need of God. God sent his only Son to share with each of us a message of salvation and eternal life with the Father in heaven. That alone is incredible. His son Jesus taught the disciples all that the Father had sent him to teach. The Apostles passed along God's message, which has been handed down from generation to generation. That, too, is incredible. That is our apostolic Christian faith, and it is our turn to pass it on.

When I walk into church on Sunday mornings, my eyes are directed to the candles on the Lord's Table and the cross of Christ just beyond. As the congregation gathers, I start to feel the profound presence of the Lord. The Body of Christ is real and tangible, and in my own way I am now a part of something very special. The music starts with the singing of the processional hymn, and as I see the cross coming down the center aisle, I am humbled knowing that Christ died on the cross for you and me. As the service progresses I am drawn closer to the presence of the Lord by the readings of Scripture, prayers, and song. I am able to repent and confess my sins directly to Jesus himself. He absolves me of my sins and my heart, mind, and soul are prepared to receive Holy Communion. By faith I am in the presence of Jesus as I receive the bread and wine. It is a very spiritual time for me as I experience His presence. I know He is with me, and by the power of the Holy Spirit I am being prepared to face the world outside the church walls. I am ready to walk out through the servant's entrance and serve Him.

Yes, I get excited about being an Anglican because it is an incredible authentic apostolic strand of Christianity given to us by God. I want to share what I have been given so others can come to experience the same excitement.

What Am I Supposed to Do?

As informed Anglicans we ought to feel that we should share what we have learned and love about our Anglican Church. Hopefully you have deepened your faith and developed a closer relationship with Jesus Christ as a result of your journey. It is time to step out in faith and pray about who the Holy Spirit is leading you to invite to church. I like what Pastor Neal Jeffrey[31] said at a recent Anglican Men's Weekend in Southern California: "Dream big, believe with your heart, show up and make the play." The last part is really important: to "show up and make the play."

Pray for the Lord's direction as to whom you will invite to church. When a name pops up (and it will), be sure to tell him or her a little about your faith and your love of being an Anglican. Be bold and know you are empowered by the Holy Spirit to complete your mission. During the next few weeks, think about those you come in contact with. Make a list of those you want to invite. Consider family members, friends, neighbors, and colleagues at work. Who might be that person you had thought about inviting to church but just haven't followed through with? Now might be the perfect time to invite that person. And others!

> Be bold and know you are empowered by the Holy Spirit to complete your mission.

If the person you ask seems a little negative, don't be discouraged, just keep going with respect and boldness and remember that at times that persistence pays off. We need to be like the Energizer Bunny that keeps going, and going, and going until the right person hears with their heart. Keep in mind that lots of folks refused to hear what Jesus and the Apostles had to say. For each person you contact, you are then and there planting a seed for the Lord or watering a seed that someone else had planted earlier. It is the Lord who will make the seed grow according to His timing (1 Corinthians 3:6).

When someone accepts your invitation to church, make sure they know the location and time of services. If you can, offer to pick them up and drive them to church and perhaps take them to lunch afterwards. Familiarize your guest in general terms with the order of the Anglican service and the Book of Common Prayer so they can follow the flow of the service. Make sure they understand why only baptized Christians may receive communion. If there's an opportunity to introduce your guest to the congregation, be sure to do so, and introduce him or her to your friends and your rector or pastor. Nothing is more welcoming to a visitor than being made to feel a part of your church family. Let them know you hope to see them next Sunday. It is a good idea to give your guest a phone call during the following week to see if they have any questions about their visit and to reinforce the invitation to attend church the next Sunday. In other words, give them the best of our Anglican hospitality! In doing so you act as an ambassador for Christ.

Session Seven
Small Group Activity

I Can Do It!

Here is a fun activity that will help prepare you for your reaching out adventure and becoming a fisher of men and women. Review from Session One the five reasons why you are an Anglican and your written Personal Reflection on "Why do I love the Anglican Church?" These two components will help build a foundation on which to build your sharing about your faith and the Anglican Church. It is best not to share what you think the other person might like to hear, but rather what you have found to be true for you. Simply share from the heart, with love, about your faith and about the Anglican Church.

Our role-playing activity should be fun and a challenge at the same time. Break up your small group into groups of two or three people in preparation for this activity. (For any who don't feel comfortable with the idea of role-playing, you should know that is exactly what presidential candidates do to prepare for questions that may come up during a debate. Law firms do it to prepare lawyer for an important argument.)

1. Take five minutes to role-play what could come up when inviting your guest to church. Take turns being the ambassador for Christ and the person being invited, a potential but reluctant guest. At the end of five minutes, each person should jot down their thoughts about their experience.

2. Change roles and repeat the role-playing for another five minutes. At the end of the time, take five minutes once again to jot down your thoughts about the experience. Everyone in the group needs to have a chance to role-play inviting a friend to church.

3. When you are finished, share with one another how you felt about the activity, what worked, and what did not work. What would make you a better ambassador for Christ? Be honest with each other, but be gentle.

4. Share the highlights of your role-playing experience with the larger group if time permits.

You might also want to switch partners and role-play again. That's up to your group, but it will help to build your confidence and organize your thoughts as you prepare like an athlete to "show up and make the play."

God's Call to Us

Anglicanism *is* simply a container for Christian truth that has been passed along from generation to generation. The *original and continuing apostolic* Christian faith is what the Church has always believed for all times! That is what we Anglicans believe. As Anglicans we have so much to cherish in the authentic Christianity delivered to the saints and passed on to us, our wonderful history, our Bible-based liturgy, and our Anglican traditions. It is our responsibility as ambassadors

> Anglicanism *is* simply a container for Christian truth that has been passed along from generation to generation.

for Christ to pass on to our family, friends, colleagues, and community the good news that they too can have a personal relationship with Jesus Christ. In doing so we have the opportunity to share the Anglican way, which is nothing other than the faith of the original Apostles, nothing added and nothing subtracted. And be sure that they understand that for Anglicans the Bible—Holy Scripture—reigns supreme!

With Jesus as our Lord and Savior, and having made a decision to serve Him by giving ourselves up into His service, we are obligated to share our Christianity with others. That is God's call to us.

This is the moment to reach out and help build God's Kingdom on earth.

What Will You Do?

As Jesus said to his disciples Simon and Andrew, "Come, follow me and I will make you fishers of men. And immediately they left their nets and followed him" (Mark 1:17-18 ESV).

Jesus, who is the same yesterday, today and yes, forever, is saying the same thing to us today as he did to His first disciples.

Let us leave our nets, follow Him, and become fishers of men. Amen

Appendix A

The Apostles' Creed

I believe in God, the Father almighty,
creator of heaven and earth.
I believe in Jesus Christ, his only Son, our Lord.
He was conceived by the power of the Holy Spirit
and born of the Virgin Mary.
He suffered under Pontius Pilate,
was crucified, died, and was buried.
He descended to the dead.
On the third day he rose again.
He ascended into heaven,
and is seated at the right hand of the Father.
He will come again to judge the living and the dead.
I believe in the Holy Spirit,
the holy catholic Church,
the communion of saints,
the forgiveness of sins,
the resurrection of the body,
and the life everlasting. Amen

Appendix B

The Creed of Saint Athanasius

Whosoever will be saved, before all things it is necessary that he hold the Catholic Faith.

Which Faith except everyone do keep whole and undefiled, without doubt he shall perish everlastingly.

And the Catholic Faith is this: That we worship one God in Trinity, and Trinity in Unity, neither confounding the Persons, nor dividing the Substance.

For there is one Person of the Father, another of the Son, and another of the Holy Ghost.

But the Godhead of the Father, of the Son and of the Holy Ghost, is all one, the Glory equal, the Majesty co-eternal.

Such as the Father is, such is the Son, and such is the Holy Ghost.

The Father uncreate, the Son uncreate, and the Holy Ghost uncreate.

The Father incomprehensible, the Son incomprehensible, and the Holy Ghost incomprehensible. The Father eternal, the Son eternal, and the Holy Ghost eternal.

And yet they are not three eternals, but one eternal.

As also there are not three incomprehensibles, nor three uncreated, but one uncreated, and one incomprehensible.

So likewise the Father is Almighty, the Son Almighty, and the Holy Ghost Almighty.

And yet they are not three Almighties but one Almighty.

So the Father is God, the Son is God, and the Holy Ghost is God.

And yet they are not three Gods, but one God.

So likewise the Father is Lord, the Son Lord, and the Holy Ghost Lord.

And yet not three Lords but one Lord.

For, like as we are compelled by the Christian verity to acknowledge every Person by Himself to be God and Lord,

So are we forbidden by the Catholic Religion to say, There be three Gods or three Lords. The Father is made of none, neither created, nor begotten.

The Son is of the Father alone, not made, nor created, but begotten.

The Holy Ghost is of the Father, and of the Son neither made, nor created, nor begotten, but proceeding.

So there is One Father, not three Fathers; one Son, not three Sons; one Holy Ghost, not three Holy Ghosts.

And in this Trinity none is afore or after other; none is greater or less than another;

But the whole three Persons are co-eternal together, and co-equal.

So that in all things, as is aforesaid, the Unity in Trinity, and the Trinity in Unity, is to be worshipped.

He therefore that will be saved, must thus think of the Trinity.

Furthermore, it is necessary to everlasting salvation, that he also believe rightly the Incarnation of our Lord Jesus Christ.

For the right Faith is, that we believe and confess, that our Lord Jesus Christ, the Son of God, is God and Man.

God, of the substance of the Father, begotten before the worlds; and Man, of the substance of His mother, born into the world;

Perfect God and perfect Man, of a reasonable Soul and human Flesh subsisting;

Equal to the Father as touching His Godhead, and inferior to the Father, as touching His Manhood.

Who although He be God and Man, yet He is not two, but One Christ;

One, not by conversion of the Godhead into Flesh, but by taking of the Manhood into God;

One altogether, not by confusion of Substance, but by unity of Person.

For as the reasonable soul and flesh is one Man, so God and Man is one Christ;

Who suffered for our salvation, descended into hell, rose again the third day from the dead.

He ascended into Heaven, He sitteth on the right hand of the Father, God Almighty, from whence he shall come to judge the quick and the dead.

At whose coming all men shall rise again with their bodies, and shall give account for their own works.

And they that have done good shall go into life everlasting; and they that have done evil into everlasting fire.

This is the Catholic Faith, which except a man believe faithfully and firmly, he cannot be saved.

Appendix C

The Nicene Creed

We believe in one God,
    the Father, the Almighty,
    maker of heaven and earth,
    of all that is, visible and invisible.

We believe in one Lord, Jesus Christ,
    the only Son of God,
    eternally begotten of the Father,
    God from God, Light from Light,
    true God from true God,
    begotten, not made,
    of one Being with the Father;
    through him all things were made.
    For us and for our salvation he came down from heaven,
    was incarnate from the Holy Spirit and the Virgin Mary,
    and was made man.
    For our sake he was crucified under Pontius Pilate;
    he suffered death and was buried.
    On the third day he rose again in accordance with the
    Scriptures;
    he ascended into heaven
    and is seated at the right hand of the Father.
    He will come again in glory to judge the living and the dead,
    and his kingdom will have no end.

We believe in the Holy Spirit, the Lord, the giver of life,
    who proceeds from the Father and the Son,
    who with the Father and the Son he is worshiped and
    glorified,
    who has spoken through the prophets.
    We believe in one holy catholic and apostolic Church.
    We acknowledge one baptism for the forgiveness of sins.
    We look for the resurrection of the dead,
    and the life of the world to come. Amen.

Appendix D

The Constitution of
The Anglican Church in North America

AS ratified by the Provincial Assembly, June 2009 and amended by the Provincial Assembly, June 2012

PREAMBLE

In the Name of God, the Father, the Son and the Holy Spirit, Amen.

- We are Anglicans in North America united by our faith in the Lord Jesus Christ and the trustworthiness of the Holy Scriptures and presently members of the Common Cause Partnership.

- We know ourselves to be members of the One, Holy, Catholic, and Apostolic Church.

- We are grieved by the current state of brokenness within the Anglican Communion prompted by those who have embraced erroneous teaching and who have rejected a repeated call to repentance.

- We repent ourselves of things done and left undone that have contributed to or tolerated the rise of false teaching, and we humbly embrace the forgiveness that comes through Christ's atoning sacrifice.

- We are grateful for the encouragement of Primates of the worldwide Anglican Communion who gathered at Jerusalem in June 2008 and called on us to establish a new Province in North America. We affirm the Global Anglican Future Conference (GAFCON) Statement and Jerusalem Declaration issued 29 June 2008.

- We believe that this Constitution is faithful to that call and consistent with the Historic Faith and Order of the Church, and we invite the prayers of all faithful Anglicans as we seek to be obedient disciples of Jesus Christ our One Lord and Savior.

ARTICLE I:
FUNDAMENTAL DECLARATIONS OF THE PROVINCE

As the Anglican Church in North America (the Province), being a part of the One, Holy, Catholic, and Apostolic Church of Christ, we believe and confess Jesus Christ to be the Way, the Truth, and the Life: no one comes to the Father but by Him. Therefore, we identify the following seven elements as characteristic of the Anglican Way, and essential for membership:

1. We confess the canonical books of the Old and New Testaments to be the inspired Word of God, containing all things necessary for salvation, and to be the final authority and unchangeable standard for Christian faith and life.

2. We confess Baptism and the Supper of the Lord to be Sacraments ordained by Christ Himself in the Gospel, and thus to be ministered with unfailing use of His words of institution and of the elements ordained by Him.

3. We confess the godly historic Episcopate as an inherent part of the apostolic faith and practice, and therefore as integral to the fullness and unity of the Body of Christ.

4. We confess as proved by most certain warrants of Holy Scripture the historic faith of the undivided church as declared in the three Catholic Creeds: the Apostles', the Nicene, and the Athanasian.

5. Concerning the seven Councils of the undivided Church, we affirm the teaching of the first four Councils and the Christological clarifications of the fifth, sixth and seventh Councils, in so far as they are agreeable to the Holy Scriptures.

6. We receive The Book of Common Prayer as set forth by the Church of England in 1662, together with the Ordinal attached to the same, as a standard for Anglican doctrine and discipline, and, with the Books which preceded it, as the standard for the Anglican tradition of worship.

7. We receive the Thirty-Nine Articles of Religion of 1571, taken in their literal and grammatical sense, as expressing the Anglican response to certain doctrinal issues controverted at that time, and as expressing fundamental principles of authentic Anglican belief.

In all these things, the Anglican Church in North America is determined by the help of God to hold and maintain, as the Anglican Way has received them, the doctrine, discipline and worship of Christ and to transmit the same, unimpaired, to our posterity.

We seek to be and remain in full communion with all Anglican Churches, Dioceses and Provinces that hold and maintain the Historic Faith, Doctrine, Sacraments and Discipline of the One, Holy, Catholic, and Apostolic Church.

ARTICLE II:
THE MEMBERSHIP OF THE PROVINCE

1. The founding entities of the Anglican Church in North America are the members of the Common Cause Partnership namely:
    The American Anglican Council
    The Anglican Coalition in Canada
    The Anglican Communion Network
    The Anglican Mission in the Americas
    The Anglican Network in Canada
    The Convocation of Anglicans in North America
    Forward in Faith – North America
    The Missionary Convocation of Kenya
    The Missionary Convocation of the Southern Cone
    The Missionary Convocation of Uganda

The Reformed Episcopal Church

2. New dioceses, clusters or networks (whether regional or affinity-based) may be added to the Province by the Provincial Council, pursuant to the process outlined by canon.

3. Member dioceses (or groups of dioceses organized into distinct jurisdictions) are free to withdraw from the Province by action of their own governing bodies at any time.

ARTICLE III:
THE MISSION OF THE PROVINCE

1. The mission of the Province is to extend the Kingdom of God by so presenting Jesus Christ in the power of the Holy Spirit that people everywhere will come to put their trust in God through Him, know Him as Savior and serve Him as Lord in the fellowship of the Church. The chief agents of this mission to extend the Kingdom of God are the people of God.

2. The work of the Province is to equip each member of the Province so that they may reconcile the world to Christ, plant new congregations, and make disciples of all nations; baptizing them in the Name of the Father, and of the Son and of the Holy Spirit, and teaching them to obey everything commanded by Jesus Christ.

3. The Province will seek to represent orthodox North American Anglicans in the councils of the Anglican Communion.

ARTICLE IV:
THE STRUCTURE OF THE PROVINCE

1. The fundamental agency of mission in the Province is the local congregation.

2. Congregations and clergy are related together in a diocese, cluster, or network (whether regional or affinity-based), united by a bishop.

3. Each diocese, cluster or network (whether regional or affinity-based) shall be represented in the Provincial Assembly.

4. Dioceses, clusters or networks (whether regional or affinity-based) may

band together for common mission, or as distinct jurisdictions at the sub-Provincial level.

5. Each bishop in active episcopal ministry shall be included in a Provincial College of Bishops as provided by canon.

6. There shall be a Provincial Council as provided by Article VII and by Canon.

7. This Constitution recognizes the right of each diocese, cluster or network (whether regional or affinity-based) to establish and maintain its own governance, constitution and canons not inconsistent with the provisions of the Constitution and Canons of this Province.

ARTICLE V:
AREAS OF PROVINCIAL RESPONSIBILITY

The Provincial Council, subject to ratification by the Provincial Assembly, has power to make canons ordering our common life in respect to the following matters:

1. Safeguarding the Faith and Order of the Province
2. Supporting the mission of the Province
3. Common Worship
4. Standards for ordination
5. Clergy support and discipline
6. Ecumenical and international relations
7. Norms for Holy Matrimony
8. Providing for the proper administration of the Province

ARTICLE VI:
THE PROVINCIAL ASSEMBLY

1. The chief work of the Provincial Assembly shall be strengthening the mission of the Province.

2. The Provincial Assembly shall ratify Constitutional amendments and Canons adopted by the Provincial Council. The process of ratification is set forth by canon.

3. The Provincial Assembly shall be composed of representatives of all the dioceses, clusters and networks (whether regional or affinity-based) in balance and in number from the laity, bishops and other clergy as from time-to-time determined by canon.

4. The Provincial Assembly may meet as often as annually, but shall meet not less than everyfive years. Meetings shall be called as provided for by canon.

ARTICLE VII:
THE PROVINCIAL COUNCIL

1. The Provincial Council is the governing body for the Anglican Church in North America and shall have the authority to adopt canons and constitutional amendments for ratification by the Provincial Assembly and to establish the program and budget of the Province.

2. The membership of Provincial Council shall be composed as provided for by Canon. Initially, the Provincial Council shall be composed of the members of the Common Cause Leadership council, as constituted under the Common Cause Articles.

3. Provincial Council members hold office for five years. However, initially, each diocese shall take steps to implement a system of staggered terms.

4. A retiring member of the Provincial Council is eligible for re-election for one additional term, but not for a third.

5. The Provincial Council may appoint up to six persons as full members.

6. The Provincial Council may appoint a deputy chair, a secretary, a treasurer and such other office bearers as it deems necessary.

7. The Provincial Council will meet at least once in each calendar year.

8. Special meetings of the Provincial Council may be called as provided for by canon.

9. The Chair with the assistance of the Executive Committee and other office bearers will be responsible for the agenda of each Provincial Council meeting.

10. The Provincial Council shall have an Executive Committee, whose membership and duties may be established by canon. Initially the Executive Committee shall be composed of the members of the Common Cause Executive Committee, as constituted under the Common Cause Articles.

ARTICLE VIII:
THE LIMITS OF PROVINCIAL AUTHORITY

1. The member dioceses, clusters or networks (whether regional or affinity-based) and those dioceses banded together as jurisdictions shall each retain all authority they do not yield to the Province by their own consent. The powers not delegated to the Province by this constitution nor prohibited by this Constitution to these dioceses or jurisdictions, are reserved to these dioceses or jurisdictions respectively.

2. The Province shall make no canon abridging the authority of any member dioceses, clusters or networks (whether regional or affinity-based) and those dioceses banded together as jurisdictions with respect to its practice regarding the ordination of women to the diaconate or presbyterate.

ARTICLE IX:
THE ARCHBISHOP

1. The Archbishop will be known as the *Archbishop and Primate of the Anglican Church in North America*. The Archbishop will be elected by the College of Bishops.

2. The person elected as Archbishop will hold office for a term of five years concluding at the end of the meeting of the College of Bishops which elects the next Archbishop. An Archbishop who has served one term of office may be elected for a second term of office but not a third. Initially, the Moderator of the Common Cause Partnership shall serve as Archbishop and Primate of the Province.

3. The Archbishop convenes the meetings of the Provincial Assembly, Provincial Council and College of Bishops, represents the Province

in the Councils of the Church and carries out such other duties and responsibilities as may be provided by canon.

ARTICLE X:
COLLEGE OF BISHOPS

1. The chief work of the College of Bishops shall be the propagation and defense of the Faith and Order of the Church, and in service as the visible sign and expression of the Unity of the Church.
2. Each bishop in active episcopal ministry shall be included in the College of Bishops as provided by canon.
3. The College of Bishops shall elect the Archbishop from among its members.
4. The College of Bishops will meet with such frequency as best serves its chief work, and at the call of the Archbishop or one quarter of the episcopal members of the Provincial Council.
5. The College of Bishops shall have authority in the election of bishops of the Province which may be: a) consent to an election from a diocese, cluster or network (whether regional or affinity-based), or b) the actual choice and consent from among two or more nominees put forward by a diocese, cluster or network (whether regional or affinity-based), in the manner set forward by canon.

ARTICLE XI:
PROVINCIAL TRIBUNAL AND OTHER COURTS

1. There shall be an ecclesiastical court of final decision to be known as the Provincial Tribunal consisting of seven members, both lay and clergy, who shall be appointed by the Provincial Council on such terms and conditions as determined by canon. The jurisdiction of the Provincial Tribunal shall be to determine matters in dispute arising from the Constitution and Canons of the Province and such other matters as may be authorized by canon.
2. There shall be a Court for the Trial of a Bishop to function as provided by canon.

3. The Provincial Council may, by canon, create such additional courts, inferior to the Provincial Tribunal, as may be necessary or appropriate to determine matters of church discipline.

4. Each Diocese shall, by canon, establish its own ecclesiastical Trial Court for the trial of a deacon or presbyter.

ARTICLE XII:
OWNERSHIP OF PROPERTY

All church property, both real and personal, owned by each member congregation now and in the future is and shall be solely and exclusively owned by each member congregation and shall not be subject to any trust interest in favor of the Province or any other claim of ownership arising out of the canon law of this Province. Where property is held in a different manner by any diocese or grouping, such ownership shall be preserved

ARTICLE XIII:
FINANCES

Each member diocese, cluster or network (whether regional or affinity-based) or any group of dioceses organized into a distinct jurisdiction agrees to share the cost of operating the Province as provided by canon.

ARTICLE XIV:
REMOVAL FROM MEMBERSHIP

As may be provided by canon, a member diocese, cluster or network (whether regional or affinity-based) or any group of dioceses organized into a distinct jurisdiction may be removed from membership in the Province, after due warning from the Executive Committee, if agreed to by two-thirds of the members present and voting and at least a majority in two of the three orders of bishops, clergy and laity within the Provincial Council.

ARTICLE XV:
ADOPTION AND AMENDMENT
OF THIS CONSTITUTION

1. This Constitution has been adopted by the Leadership Council of the Common Cause Partnership serving as initial Provincial Council. It shall be submitted to the Provincial Assembly for ratification at a meeting to be called by the Provincial Council not later than 31 August 2009 and shall become effective immediately upon such ratification.

2. This Constitution may be amended by the Provincial Assembly by two-thirds of the members present and voting at any regular or special meeting called for that purpose. Any changes or amendments to the Constitution shall not become effective in less than ninety days following that meeting.

We certify that the foregoing is the text of the Constitution of the Anglican Church in North America adopted by the Common Cause Leadership Council functioning as the Provincial Council and ratified with amendments by the Provincial Assembly at its meeting at Saint Vincent's Cathedral, Bedford, Texas, on the 22nd day of June in the Year of our Lord 2009.

The Right Reverend Robert W. Duncan Archbishop of the Anglican Church in North America	The Venerable Charlie Masters Acting Deputy Chair and Bishop-Elect

I certify that the text of the Constitution set out above is the text of the Constitution of the Anglican Church in North America ratified by the Provincial Assembly at its meeting at Saint Vincent's Cathedral, Bedford, Texas, on the 22nd day of June in the Year of Our Lord 2009.

The Rev. Travis S. Boline
Acting Secretary

Appendix E

The Oxford Statement

The Oxford Statement: Introduction

The leaders of the GAFCON movement are keenly aware of the crises of conscience that are pressing some people to shift their membership and ministry from the Anglican Church.

While we are greatly sympathetic that there are many areas of crisis that assault conscience, once again, we would offer that the theological clarity of the Jerusalem Declaration offers a solid foundation on which to engage with other Anglicans in the pursuit of Gospel mission.

Being able to link with those who not only form the majority of Anglicans in the world, but also those who affirm biblical theological foundations of what Anglicans have always believed and practiced can provide concrete relationships and meaningful partnerships that are of more substance than the structures that have shown themselves to be flawed or compromised.

GAFCON provides a way to share biblical Anglicanism that is in concert with what Anglicans have always believed, taught, and practiced.

We believe that Anglicanism has a great deal to offer in the pursuit of reaching the world for Christ. While we wish those who are departing the Anglican Church well, we do not believe that it is necessary to depart from what Anglicans have always believed to remain faithful. At the same time, we understand that some structures have become so compromised that some have been pressed by conscience to separate from their national structures - such as in North America.

We are glad that GAFCON exists and provides links to remain Anglican when people have been unable, for conscience, to remain in their Province.

In England (as well as other areas), we invite people to re-affirm what we have always believed in Anglicanism by adopting the Jerusalem

Declaration as a statement of their own faith and join with us in partnership in working to win the world to Christ.

Statement

1. The GAFCON/FCA Primates' Council met in Oxford from October 4th through October 7th, 2010. We gathered as Bishops in Council and as the elected leaders of provinces and national churches of the Anglican Communion representing more than forty million Anglicans. We know that many of our people confront a fallen world where sin abounds; the economy is troubled and resources are scarce; disasters loom and governments often seem impotent and helpless and yet even in the midst of all these things "our hope is in the Name of the Lord" and we are filled with hope and vision.

2. We are thankful for God's hand in establishing GAFCON and the Fellowship of Confessing Anglicans. We rejoice in God's guidance from the Scriptures, the gift of the Holy Spirit to strengthen us, and the provision of a godly fellowship to sustain us. In this context we have met in Oxford, a city that has seen many critical events in Anglican history, and are grateful for the men and women who have given their lives to protect the faith that has given us eternal life.

3. We believe that we are now entering a new era for the Anglican Communion. New ways of living out our common life are emerging as old structures are proven to be ineffective in confronting the challenges of living in a pluralistic global community. We rejoice in the call of the Jerusalem Declaration for a renewed commitment to the authority of Scripture and the centrality of the gospel of Jesus Christ. Sadly the rejection of these historic anchors to our faith has brought us to a crisis in the life of the Communion.

4. As we have made clear in numerous communiqués and meetings those who have abandoned the historic teaching of the Church have torn the fabric of our life together at its deepest level. We have made repeated attempts to bring repentance and restoration and yet these efforts have been rejected. We grieve for those who have walked apart and earnestly pray for them and the people under their care.

5. For the sake of Christ and of His Gospel we can no longer maintain the illusion of normalcy and so we join with other Primates from the Global South in declaring that we will not be present at the next Primates' meeting to be held in Ireland. And while we acknowledge that the efforts to heal our brokenness through the introduction of an Anglican Covenant were well intentioned we have come to the conclusion the current text is fatally flawed and so support for this initiative is no longer appropriate.

6. We also acknowledge with appreciation the address to the Nicean Society meeting in Lambeth Palace on September 9th of His Eminence, Metropolitan Hilarion of Volokolamsk, Chairman of the Moscow Patriarchate's Department for External Church Relations. We welcome his call to all churches of the Anglican Communion to step back from the abyss of heresy and reclaim the revealed truth that is at the heart of our historic understanding of Christian faith and moral order. We share with him the conviction that failure to do so will endanger our common witness and many important ecumenical dialogues but we would also point out that there are many within the Anglican Communion who have not 'bowed the knee' to secular liberalism and who are determined to stay true to the 'faith once delivered to the saints' whatever the cost.

7. The Primates Council, as bishops of the One, Holy, Catholic and Apostolic Church, wish to affirm the reality of human sin and divine judgment, the only way of salvation from sin through the death of the Lord Jesus Christ on the cross, the sufficiency and clarity of Holy Scripture as the revelation of God's will, and the transforming power of the Holy Spirit as he brings new birth and holiness of life.

8. As many people in the nations where we serve experience new economic

challenges, we affirm that the Church has been entrusted with the task of holding before all people the truth of the gospel of the kingdom of God revealed in Jesus Christ, the key to human well-being and the hope of creation. While we know well the scourge of poverty and the despair it produces, we call on our churches to remember this unique calling and not be seduced by those who would argue that economic development is our only goal. The destiny of humanity is not limited to this present world but to live the resurrection life in the new heavens and new earth.

9. We are, however, determined to lead our churches away from unhealthy economic dependency and to teach our people the importance of becoming effective stewards of their own resources. We must reclaim a vision of financial self-sufficiency. We are grateful for reports of several initiatives that are building capacity for economic growth in our various provinces and commit ourselves to making this an essential dimension of our continuing work. We also believe that a vital part of our witness is the integrity of our marriages and families and our care for the most vulnerable among us, our children. We welcome recent initiatives to encourage the ministry of women in leadership by CAPA – the Council of Anglican Provinces in Africa.

10. We are also grateful for the recent conference sponsored by CAPA in Entebbe, Uganda, where we witnessed the growing strength of the Anglican Churches in Africa and their commitment to holistic mission. We believe that GAFCON/FCA must expand its ministry through the inclusion of other Anglican provinces that share our faith conviction and love for the Communion. We also applaud the efforts of the Global South Provinces to find common ground and opportunities for common mission. We are committed to doing all that we can to strengthen our common witness.

11. We remain convinced that the unique character of GAFCON/FCA with its diversity of cultures and its embrace of the Jerusalem Declaration as a common theological confession is a vital contribution to the future of the global Anglican Communion. We are persuaded that we must offer

new initiatives to more effectively respond to the crises that confront us all. We must strengthen our communication capabilities and we are also looking to build partnerships with other denominational churches that share our faith convictions.

12. Specifically, we are planning a leadership conference in the latter part of 2011 that will focus on the need to "Contend for the Faith in the Public Square." We are also beginning preparations for an international gathering of Primates, Bishops, Clergy and Lay leaders in 2012, provisionally designated "GAFCON 2." To support all of this we have approved the expansion of the Secretariat.

13. Finally, we acknowledge that it is only by God's grace that we can accomplish any of this and so we call on all those that acknowledge Jesus Christ as Lord to join us in prayer for our world and for the raising up of many initiatives that will bring the redeeming and transforming love of God to all those in need.

14. To him who is able to keep you from falling and to present you before his glorious presence without fault and with great joy — to the only God our Savior be glory, majesty, power and authority, through Jesus Christ our Lord, before all ages, now and forevermore! Amen."

Appendix F

The Nairobi Commitment

We are committed to Jesus Christ as the head of the Church, the authority of his Word and the power of his gospel. The Son perfectly reveals God to us, he is the sole ground of our salvation, and he is our hope for the future. We seek to honor him, walk in faith and obedience to his teaching, and glorify him through our proclamation of his name.

Therefore, in the power of the Holy Spirit:

1. We commit ourselves anew to The Jerusalem Statement and Declaration.

2. We commit ourselves to supporting mission, both locally and globally, including outreach to Muslims. We also commit to encouraging lay training in obedience to the Great Commission to make and mature disciples, with particular attention to recruiting and mobilizing young people for ministry and leadership.

3. We commit ourselves to give greater priority to theological education and to helping each other find the necessary resources. The purposes of theological education need clarifying so that students are better oriented to ministry, faculty are well-trained, and curricula are built on the faithful reading of Scripture.

4. We commit ourselves to defend essential truths of the biblical faith even when this defense threatens existing structures of human authority (Acts 5:29). For this reason, the bishops at GAFCON 2013 resolved 'to affirm and endorse the position of the Primates' Council in providing oversight in cases where provinces and dioceses compromise biblical faith, including the affirmation of a duly discerned call to ministry. This may involve ordination and consecration if the situation requires.

5. We commit ourselves to the support and defense of those who in standing for apostolic truth are marginalized or excluded from formal communion with other Anglicans in their dioceses. We have therefore recognized the Anglican Mission in England (AMiE) as an expression of authentic Anglicanism both for those within and outside the Church of England, and welcomed their intention to appoint a General Secretary of AMiE.

6. We commit ourselves to teach about God's good purposes in marriage and in singleness. Marriage is a life-long exclusive union between a man and a woman. We exhort all people to work and pray for the building and strengthening of healthy marriages and families. For this reason, we oppose the secular tide running in favor of cohabitation and same-sex marriage.

7. We commit ourselves to work for the transformation of society though the gospel. We repudiate all violence, especially against women and children; we shall work for the economic empowerment of those who are deprived; and we shall be a voice for persecuted Christians.

8. We commit ourselves to the continuation of the Global Fellowship of Confessing Anglicans, putting membership, staffing and financing onto a new basis. We shall continue to work within the Anglican Communion for its renewal and reform.

9. We commit ourselves to meet again at the next GAFCON.

Now to him who is able to do far more abundantly than all that we ask or think, according to the power at work within us, to him be glory in the church and in Christ Jesus throughout all generations, forever and ever. Amen. (Ephesians 3:20-21)

Appendix G

Recommended Readings for Further Study

Chan, Francis. *Forgotten God, Reversing our Tragic Neglect of the Holy Spirit*. Colorado Springs, CO: David C. Cook Publishing, 2009.

Collins, Chuck. *Cranmer's Church: Introducing the Episcopal Church and Anglicanism in America*. San Antonio, TX: The Watercress Press, 2005.

Green, Michael. *Thirty Years That Changed the World*. Grand Rapids, MI: Wm. B. Eerdmans Publishing Co., 2004.

Lewis, C.S. *Mere Christianity*. New York: Macmillan Publishing Co., Inc., 1977.

Moorman, JRH. *A History of the Church in England*. Harrisburg, PA: Morehouse Publishing, 1980.

Null, Ashley. "Thomas Cranmer's Theology of the Heart." Lecture at St. Andrew's

Cathedral, Sydney, Australia, April 2006.

Okoh, Nicholas, et al. *Being Faithful: The Shape of Historic Anglicanism Today*. London: Latimer Trust, 2008.

Packer, J.I. *Concise Theology: A Guide to Historic Christian Beliefs*. Carol Stream, IL: Tyndale House Publishers, Inc., 1993.

Spencer, Bonnell. *Ye Are The Body: A People's History of the Church*. West Part, NY: Holy Cross Publications, 1976.

Stott, John. *Basic Christianity*. Downer Grove, IL: IVP Books, 2006.

Sykes, Booty, and Knight. *The Study of Anglicanism*. Minneapolis, MN: Fortress Press, 1999.

Appendix H

A Prayer to Receive Jesus Christ as Your Savior
(Sinner's Prayer)

The Apostle Paul writes:

If you confess with your mouth that Jesus is Lord and believe in your heart that God raised him from the dead, you will be saved. (Romans 10:9)

God never forces his way into our lives. Each of us must individually make the decision to invite Jesus to come into our heart and be part of our everyday life. If you are ready to start a relationship with God, then say the following prayer to invite Jesus Christ to come into your heart, and then receive Him as your Lord and Savior.

> Lord Jesus, I need you.
>
> Thank you for dying on the cross for me.
>
> Forgive me of my sins and come into my life.
>
> I receive You as my Savior and Lord.
>
> Thank You for forgiving me and giving me eternal life.
>
> Fill me with Your Holy Spirit.
>
> Help me be the person God made me to be.
>
> I ask these things in Your Name, Amen.

Note: This prayer is for the purpose of leading an individual to Christ. If you do lead an individual to Christ, be sure to invite them to church with you the following Sunday. Of course you should share the news with your rector or pastor.

Appendix I

Secrets for Group Leaders

If your congregation plans to divide into small groups to study *Celebrate Anglicanism,* we recommend that the rector appoint a lay leader for each small group. The lay leaders should review these "secrets" in order to understand their role as facilitator. First and foremost, the group leader is not to teach, preach, critique, or analyze while leading a group. Simply facilitate. The tips that follow are not new, but they allow for smooth small group sessions.

It is strongly recommended that if a group is to meet in a home, it should be the home of a group member other than the facilitator, who needs to be free of the distractions of hosting. It also opens that role for another.

1. Welcome people to the group with a smile and thank them for attending. Suggest that it is important to complete their homework and attend each week for discussion and sharing time. Get them to see that they are in the group for a reason, and that unless they make the commitment to see it through, they could be depriving the group of what the Lord may be able to bring out through them.

2. Open your group with a short prayer and ask for the Holy Spirit's presence as you tackle the Questions for Preparation and Discussion.

3. Have everyone introduce themselves to the group, and suggest that they limit their introductions to 30 seconds. Ask them to simply share their name and what church or which service they attend. Start the ball rolling by introducing yourself in even less than 30 seconds!

4. Nametags are very helpful and should be visible. They really help in getting to know one another for at least the first couple of sessions.

5. Ensure the group that confidentiality is a part of the group's operation. Any sharing or discussion of a personal nature stays in the group.

6. Keep the group focused on the question at hand. Recall that it is not a time to teach, preach, critique, or analyze! Your job isn't to be the leader you are at church (although that is why you were chosen). You only *facilitate.* That means you keep things pretty much on track, you

get the others talking, and you make sure no one dominates.

7. Don't be alarmed if you experience a long period of silence when you ask a question. Give it time and someone will respond. If all else fails, you should be prepared to share your answer.

8. Sometimes an individual will dominate the group's time together. Perhaps the person feels the need to talk for one reason or another, but you should do all you can to get everyone involved in the time allotted to the group. If necessary, talk to the person after the group meeting and remind them that others should have an opportunity to share.

9. Thank each person after they share. Ask if anyone else would like to share his or her answer. On occasion you may have a group member who doesn't share. If that is the case, talk to them in private after the meeting and let them know that what they have to share is important and will not be criticized by anyone in the group. Remember that you *do not* want to force anyone to share during the small group time. As a rule of thumb, don't "go around the circle" where everyone is forced to answer a question, with the exception of self-introductions.

10. When the group is finished with a question, move on graciously to the next one. You will have a limited amount of time so keep the group on task. However, if an important sharing is taking place, let it take its course. Try to catch up next time.

11. If for some reason an individual seems to be having a tough time with an answer, it is okay to stop and pray for them if they give permission. It may be necessary for you to consult your pastor or rector if a spiritual issue needs attention.

12. The purpose of this course is to learn about the Anglican stand of Christianity. Stay focused on Anglicanism. If a question arises that is too difficult to answer, tell the group you will try to find out the answer and talk about it the next week.

13. Last and perhaps most important, as a group leader you are not alone. God makes it very clear in Hebrews 13:5: "Never will I leave you; never will I forsake you." Be sure to ask for the Lord's help, direction, and blessing. He is waiting.

Notes

1. ACNA Canons, Title 1, Canon 10, "Of the Laity," Section 2

2. Rev. Canon Dr. Michael Green, in Chapter 5 of his book *Thirty Years That Changed the World*, discusses "What of Their Lifestyle?" Canon Green suggests that the Christian lifestyle traits of the 1st century still apply in the 21st century. He outlines 11 desirable lifestyle traits for Christians to model today.

3. An effort was made to identify those questions that were asked most often from among all the questions submitted about the Anglican Church. The answers provided here are not in-depth responses to all the questions, but they do contain a summary of fundamental information about the Anglican Church. One may wish to debate some of the answers, but from the perspective of a layperson I believe that the answers here will suffice.

4. John Stott, *Evangelical Truth* (Illinois: InterVarsity Press, 2003) 96.

5. John Stott, *Basic Christianity* (Illinois: InterVarsity Press, 2006) 105.

6. *Unger's Bible Dictionary*, s.v. "Christianity," 1983.

7. *Unger's Bible Dictionary,* s.v. "Christian," 1983.

8. Jeffrey Francis Fisher, Archbishop of Canterbury. Young Fisher attended Exeter College, Oxford (1906–11), and the Wells Theological College, becoming a deacon in 1912 and a priest in 1913. He became headmaster at Repton School (1914–32), bishop of Chester (1932–39), and then bishop of London (1939–45) at the outset of World War II. The bombings, evacuations, and general disorganizations of parish life were severe challenges, and Fisher organized a multidenominational reconstruction committee and headed a war-damage committee. He also associated himself with the Sword of the Spirit movement, seeking cooperation between the Roman Catholic Church and other churches. His administrative and organizational skills led to his appointment as Archbishop of Canterbury on January 2, 1945.

9. Bishop Jack Iker's Advent Message for 2010, "A Reflection on Our Anglican Identity" (Texas: 2010) 5.
10. Archbishop Orombi's statement may be found in a paper written in 2007 and published in the August/September 2007 edition of the ecumenical journal *First Things*
11. Ibid.
12. The Rt. Rev. Dr. Michael Nazir-Ali, Retired Bishop of Rochester (England) and President, Oxford Center for Training, Advocacy, Research and Dialogue, in a 2010 letter to Ron Speers, President of the Diocese of Western Anglicans, Anglican Church in North America.
13. The Rev. Canon Dr. Michael Green, Wycliffe Hall, Oxford; Professor, renowned evangelist, and author of more than 50 Christian books.
14. St. Aidan and St. Cuthbert

Saint Aidan

St. Aidan did a tremendous amount of missionary work, building churches and spreading Celtic Christian influence to a degree that Lindisfarne became the virtual capital of Christian England. The saint also recruited classes of Anglo-Saxon youths to be educated at Lindisfarne. Among them was Saint Eata, abbot of Melrose and later of Lindisfarne. In time, Eata's pupil, Saint Cuthbert, also became Bishop of Lindisfarne.

Aidan lived a frugal life, and encouraged the laity to fast and study the Scriptures. He himself fasted on Wednesdays and Fridays, and seldom ate at the royal table. When a feast was set before him he would give the food away to the hungry. The presents he received were given to the poor or used to buy the freedom of slaves, some of whom entered the priesthood. During Lent, Aidan would retire to the small island of Farne for prayer and penance. While there in 651, he saw smoke rising from Bamburgh, which was then under attack by the pagan King Penda of Mercia. He prayed for the wind to change, and many of the besiegers were subsequently destroyed by fire.

Saint Cuthbert

Saint Cuthbert was born in Britain about the year 635 and became a monk in his youth at the monastery of Melrose by the River Tweed. After many years of struggle as a true priest of Christ, in the service both of his own brethren and of the neglected Christians of isolated country villages, he became a solitary on Farne Island in 676. After eight years as a hermit, he was constrained to leave his quiet to become Bishop of Lindisfarne, in which office he served for almost two years. He returned to his hermitage two months before he reposed in peace in 687. Because of the miracles he was responsible for both during his life and at his tomb after his death, he is called "The Wonderworker of Britain." The whole English people honored him, and kings were both benefactors to his shrine and supplicants of his prayers. Eleven years after his death, his holy relics were revealed to be incorrupt; when his body was translated from Lindisfarne to Durham Cathedral in August of 1104, his body was still found to be untouched by decay, giving off "an odor of sweetest fragrancy," and "from the flexibility of its joints representing a person asleep rather than dead."

15. These core beliefs or characteristics of the Anglican Way are stated in Article I of the Constitution of the Anglican Church in North America as "Fundamental Declarations of the Province."

16. Archbishop Robert Duncan of the Anglican Church in North America recently made a statement that defines the Book of Common Prayer so perfectly. "The Book of Common Prayer is nothing more than the Bible organized for worship."

17. Bishop Thomas Ken, Bishop of Bath and Wells, said these words about Anglican theology on his deathbed. As a bishop he was efficient and faithful and travelled round his diocese ministering to clergy and people. He gave meticulous pastoral care to his clergy, encouraging daily services and preaching in the parish churches. At the same time he was lavish in his charitable giving to those in need, and when at

home on Sundays he always invited twelve poor people to dine with him but afterwards gave them spiritual nourishment as well.

18. Matthew Parker (1504–1575) was Archbishop of Canterbury from 1559 until his death in 1575. He was an influential theologian and arguably the cofounder of Anglican theological thought along with Thomas Cranmer and Richard Hooker. Parker was one of the primary architects of the Thirty-Nine Articles, the defining statements of Anglican doctrine.

19. The first Book of Common Prayer was prepared by Thomas Cranmer in 1549. The intent was that services and prayer would be common through the realm, to the benefit of people visiting different parishes. The moderately revised 1662 edition is regarded as the standard for the Anglican practice and remains in use in many places in the world today. In America, most Anglicans use either the 1928 BCP or the 1979 version. ACNA has a task force at work developing a version that it hopes will so highly recommend itself that it will become the accepted standard for Anglican churches in North America.

20. Historically, an oath of adherence to the Articles was a prerequisite for ordination of clergy throughout the Anglican world. The Church of England stopped the oath of adherence in 1975.

21. Charismatic style of worship is more relaxed but maintains the traditional elements of reading Scripture, preaching, and the Eucharist. At my church in Newport Beach, California, the service will have an extended period of musical praise and worship with a praise or renewal band playing contemporary Christian music. Members of the congregation often experience a strong presence of the Holy Spirit during the service. Manifestations of the Holy Spirit are often present during the service and can include healings, prophecy, or glossolalia (speaking in tongues or languages).

22. A "high church" or Anglo-Catholic service is usually a more formal liturgy celebrated by clergy in distinctive vestments. Between the extremes are a variety of styles of worship, often involving a robed choir and the use of an organ to accompany the singing of hymns and

to provide music before and after the service. Anglican churches have pews or chairs, and it is usual for the congregation to kneel for some prayers but to stand for hymns and other parts of the service such as the Gloria, Collect, Gospel reading, Creed, and either the Preface or all of the Eucharistic Prayer. High-church Anglicans may make the sign of the cross during parts of a church service. In 1845, additional Anglo-Catholic traditions were introduced and included the use of incense, candles, genuflection, vestments, intoning (chanting prayers), the title "Father", adoration of the elements of Communion, and the wearing of the clerical collar by clergy. (This caused some to depart from the Episcopal Church and form the reformed Episcopal Church as mentioned earlier.)

Until the mid-twentieth century the main Sunday service typically was Morning Prayer, but the Eucharist has once again become the standard form of Sunday worship in most Anglican churches. Other common services include an early morning Eucharist without music, an abbreviated Eucharist following a service of Morning Prayer, and a service of Evening Prayer. The late evening service of Compline was revived for parish use in the early 20th century. An Anglican service (whether or not a Eucharist) will include readings from the Bible that are generally taken from a standardized lectionary found in the Book of Common Prayer. Much of the Bible will be read out loud in the church over a three-year cycle. The sermon is typically about twenty minutes in length, though it may be much longer in Evangelical churches. Even in the most informal Evangelical services, it is common for set prayers such as the weekly collect to be read. There are also set forms for intercessory prayer, though this is now more often extemporaneous.

23. Rt. Rev Michael Nazir-Ali's address, "Jesus, Lord of His Church and of the Church's Mission," made to the Global Fellowship of Confessing Anglicans Leaders Conference at St. Mark's Battersea Rise on April 25, 2012.

24. The Book of Common Prayer (BCP) is the foundational prayer book of Anglicanism. The original book of 1549 (revised in 1552 to a

more Protestant version) was one of the instruments of the English Reformation, replacing the various rites in Latin that had been used in different parts of the country with a single compact volume in the language of the people, so that "now from henceforth all the Realm shall have but one use." Archbishop of Canterbury Thomas Cranmer wrote the first two versions of the Book of Common Prayer (1549 and 1552). The Book of Common Prayer was suppressed under Queen Mary I, but was revived when Charles II came to the throne in 1660. In 1662, the Bill of Uniformity was passed that mandated the Book of Common Prayer be used in all churches of England. From that time until now, the 1662 Book of Common Prayer has remained the standard for the Anglican Church.

With British colonial expansion from the seventeenth century onwards, the Anglican Church spread around the globe. The newly planted churches at first used the 1662 Book of Common Prayer until they, like their parent church, produced prayer books, which took into account the developments of liturgical study and practice in the nineteenth and twentieth centuries.

The 1662 English Book of Common Prayer forms the historical basis for most Anglican liturgy around the world. A revision of the 1662 Book of Common Prayer took place in America and was formally adopted in 1789 by the Protestant Episcopal Church in America. It is known today as the 1928 Book of Common Prayer. A more recent revision of the 1928 BCP by the Protestant Episcopal Church in America is known as the 1979 Book of Common Prayer.

The 1928 Book of Common Prayer is considered to be more traditional and consistent with the 1662 Book of Common Prayer than the 1979 revision. The 1979 BCP is in use by a number of Anglican churches in the United States, but it has many critics as the revisions are not considered orthodox by a number of Anglicans.

25. See note 16 above.

26. ACNA Canons, Title One, Canon 10

27. Canon Chuck Collins' reasons for infant baptism are:
    - References in the Bible emphasize God acting towards us, not us toward him. Simply said, God baptizes us into his kingdom.
    - For the first 1500 years of Christendom, it was the universal practice to baptize infants.
    - Circumcision, baptism's Old Testament antecedent, was performed on Jewish boys eight days old as a pledge and promise of Covenant blessings. This was done long before the infants could decide for themselves, yet circumcised babies were considered full members of the faith community. In the same way, baptism brings us into full membership in the New Covenant community. See Col. 2:11-12.
    - Infant baptism is the example of God's unconditional love. It's the perfect picture of God's grace. Individuals are not saved because they deserve it or have earned it. It is something God does for us as a free gift by his grace. Infants are baptized because there is no reason to withhold from them the greatest gift of all, welcoming them into the community of believers who will love them and bring them into a relationship with Jesus.

28. On Saturday, October 31, 2009, on the eve of All Saints' Day, bishops, clergy, and laity from around the United States, Canada, and Uganda gathered in Newport Beach, California, for the ordination and consecration of William Avery Thompson as the first Bishop of the Diocese of Western Anglicans. This was a great day for Anglicans on the west coast as we saw our dreams become a reality. We celebrated with a service that praised God, and all present felt the Holy Spirit come upon us that day in a mighty way. More information may be found at the Diocese of Western Anglicans web site at **www.westernanglicans.org.**

29. Sir Thomas Cromwell, 1st Earl of Essex (1485-1540), was an English statesman who served as King Henry VIII's principal secretary and chief minister from 1532 to 1540. He was a strong advocate for the English Reformation, which led to the break with the papacy in Rome. His greatest accomplish was the publication of the Great Bible as the first authoritative version in English. He later was condemned to death

without a trial and beheaded on Tower Hill on July 28, 1540.

30. In 1534 a merchant commissioned Myles Coverdale to translate the entire Bible into English. He was the first person to publish an entire Bible in the English language, the so-called Coverdale Bible, in 1535. In 1537 one of his translations included a revised edition of Tyndale's Bible, known as Matthew's Bible, the first true, direct English translation of the complete Bible. King Henry VIII wanted an authorized version of the Bible to be placed in every parish in the Church of England. It was to be read aloud at services and available to parish members. He asked Sir Thomas Cromwell to head up the task. Cromwell retained Myles Coverdale to write the Bible that later became known as the Great Bible. The task was completed in 1539. Coverdale later edited the second edition of the Great Bible published is 1540. The 2nd edition had a preface written by Thomas Cranmer, the Archbishop of Canterbury. Hence the 2nd edition of the Great Bible is referred to as the "Cranmer Bible."

    Myles Coverdale's translation of the Psalter (book of Psalms) is used in the Anglican Book of Common Prayer, and is the most familiar translation of the psalms for many Anglicans around the world.

31. Pastor Neal Jeffrey is a former All-American quarterback at Baylor University and NFL quarterback for the San Diego Chargers. He is an associate minister at Prestonwood Church of Dallas, Texas. His first book, *If I Can, Y-Y-You Can!* (Dallas, TX: Sampson Publishing, 2006), inspires men, women, and young people to achieve their highest and noblest dreams through the power of faith, belief, and action.

Glossary

Advent

The ecclesiastical (church) season that includes the four Sundays before Christmas. It is from the Latin word *adventus,* meaning *coming,* and is a season of expectant waiting and preparation for the celebration of the nativity or birth of Jesus at Christmas.

Anglican Communion

A fellowship of Anglican provinces (national or regional churches) that is based on an acknowledged commonality of Christian faith. This faith is expressed in documents like the Chicago-Lambeth Quadrilateral (1886), which lists the four non-negotiable elements of a Christian body (page 877 of the 1979 BCP), and in the Thirty-Nine Articles of Religion, as well as on an historic relationship with the Church of England and adherence to Anglican practice. The style of worship reflected in the 1662 Book of Common Prayer is prevalent in the Anglican Communion.

Anglican Orthodoxy

Anglican orthodoxy is defined by, and centered on, the church's classic formularies: the 1662 Book of Common Prayer, including the Ordinal; the Thirty-Nine Articles; and the seven early Councils of the Church, all of which uphold the authority of the Holy Bible.

Apostolic

The Anglican Church has its origins in the enduring truth of the teaching of the Apostles as recorded in Holy Scripture.

Apostolic Succession

A central pillar of the Anglican tradition is that the Apostles gave spiritual authority to bishops (overseers) to govern the Church (Acts 20:17), to confer Holy Orders on priests and deacons, and to administer the rite of Confirmation. Apostolic authority has been passed on down through the one holy, catholic, and apostolic church for 2,000 years through the consecration of a priest to the office of bishop. Through the imposition of hands by three or more bishops, the new bishop becomes a successor of the Apostles for the whole church by the grace of the Holy Spirit. The newly consecrated bishop receives a Holy Bible as a reminder that a bishop must defend the faith as a part of his responsibility.

Archbishop

The bishop who has jurisdiction over a province (a national or regional church) in the Anglican Communion.

Archbishop of Canterbury

The chief bishop and principal leader of the Church of England, the symbolic head ("first among equals") of the worldwide Anglican Communion, and the diocesan bishop of the Diocese of Canterbury. In his role as titular head of the Anglican Communion, he represents the third largest group of Christians in the world. The Archbishop of Canterbury convenes the Primates Council of the Anglican Communion, which includes the 38 primates (heads of the independent Anglican provinces). Although without legal authority outside England, he is recognized as the senior bishop of the worldwide Anglican Communion. Since 1867 he has convened a meeting of worldwide Anglican Bishops every ten years called the Lambeth Conference. In the present state of the Anglican Communion, the Archbishop of Canterbury has lost much of his influence over many of the other primates due to the continuing liberal drift of the Church of England.

Canticle

A song or hymn used to praise the Lord, with words usually taken from the Bible.

Catholic

The term *catholic* (small "c") refers to the teachings of the church that are true for all people for all times. The term refers to being a part of the ancient undivided Christian church which has remained faithful to Christian teachings from the very beginning of Christianity. The 1979 Book of Common Prayer (page 854) reads, "The Church is catholic because it proclaims the whole Faith to all people, to the end of time."

The term *catholic* is not to be confused with the Roman Catholic Church.

Church Plant

A new congregation that an existing congregation "plants" in a separate location. The ACNA Canons provide that "A congregation, with the consent of the Bishop, should plant new churches whenever possible. In such case the congregation shall provide spiritual cover and temporal assistance to the newly planted congregation until it is self-sustaining. A newly planted congregation is self-sustaining when it is able to call and provide for its own Clergy and is acceptable to the Bishop." The canons call congregations to "Commission, Provision, Bless, and Release" new church plants. ACNA has called for the planting of 1,000 new ACNA churches between 2009 and 2014 in its "*Anglican 1000*" initiative.)

Confession

An acknowledgement of sin made either in general terms by a congregation during liturgical worship, by an individual penitent in private, or in a private face-to-face confession to a priest.

Congregation

By Constitutional provision the local congregation is the fundamental agency of the mission of the Province. This is in recognition that only the local congregation (read "the local clergy and all lay persons as a team") can accomplish ACNA's mission to "Extend the Kingdom of God by so presenting Jesus Christ in the power of the Holy Spirit that people everywhere will come to put their trust in God through Him, know Him as Savior, and serve Him as Lord in the fellowship of the Church. The chief agents of this mission to extend the Kingdom of God are the people of God" (ACNA Constitution, Article III.1).

"Every congregation of the Church belongs to the Church by union with a Diocese of the Church" (ACNA Canons, Title I, 6.2). Other canonical provisions include: "Every congregation shall be established in accordance with the laws of the State or jurisdiction where situated, shall handle its own finances, and shall carry insurance coverage in amounts specified by its Diocese" (6.3). "There shall be a governing board of each congregation, often known as the vestry, which is chosen and serves according to applicable laws, diocesan canon, and the congregational by-laws. The Presbyter in charge of the congregation shall always be a member of the governing board and its presiding officer except as provided by diocesan canon. The governing board is responsible for the temporalities of the congregation and, except where otherwise provided by canon, supports the clergy in the spiritual leadership of the congregation" (6.5) "All congregational property, real and personal, owned by a member congregation shall not be subject to any trust in favor of the Province or other claim of ownership rising out of the canon law of the Church; neither may any Diocese assert any such claim over the property of any of its congregations without express written consent of the congregation" (6.5, Concerning Property Ownership). "A congregation, with the consent of the Bishop, should plant new churches whenever possible. In such case the congregation shall provide spiritual cover and temporal assistance to the newly planted congregation until it is self-sustaining. A newly planted congregation is self-sustaining when it is able to call and provide for its own Clergy and is acceptable to the Bishop" (6.7, Church Planting). (Dioceses usually have their own canons, not in conflict with ACNA's, concerning congregations and their operation.)

Collect

A short prayer that "collects" a main theme, comprised of an invocation, petition, and conclusion (usually a thanksgiving or an acknowledgement of the Deity). The collect is used before the communion service and in morning and evening prayer services. Originally, collects collected the main thought of the Bible reading for the day. Later, they concluded a place in the liturgy when the people offered up their silent prayers. However used, the collects have helped shape the belief of Anglicans for centuries.

Council

Councils (also known as General or Ecumenical Councils) are

gatherings of the whole church to discuss and come to agreement on matters of faith, morals, and discipline. Of the first seven councils of the undivided church, the Anglican Church fully accepts the teachings of the first four councils and parts of the fifth, sixth and seventh councils' teachings that are Christological clarifications and that are in agreement with Scripture. The seven Councils are the First Council of Nicea (325), First Council of Constantinople (381), Council of Ephesus (431), Council of Chalcedon (451), Second Council of Constantinople (553), Third Council of Constantinople (680-1), and the Second Council of Nicea (787).

Deacon

A Christian minister just below the Holy Order of priest. A Deacon most often serves for one year in preparation for ordination to the priesthood, although some are ordained as permanent deacons. Deacons are allowed to read the Epistle and the Gospel, but are not allowed to consecrate the elements at Communion or give absolution for sins.

Diocese

ACNA's Canons presently define a diocese this way: "A Diocese is a grouping of congregations gathered for mission under the oversight of a Bishop. A Diocese is composed of a minimum of 12 congregations with an average Sunday attendance (ASA) of at least 50 persons each and a collective ASA of at least 1,000." The "under the oversight of a bishop" part is important, as ACNA's constitution makes clear: "We confess the godly historic Episcopate as an inherent part of the apostolic faith and practice, and therefore as integral to the fullness and unity of the Body of Christ." In other words, you can't have a "Lone Ranger" Anglican congregation that isn't under the authority of a bishop. ACNA's Constitution states that "Congregations and clergy are related together in a diocese...united by a bishop" (Constitution, Article IV.2).

Episcopate

All the bishops together, or a single bishop's reign as a bishop. From the

Greek *Episkopos*, which means chief elder.

Epistle

From the Greek word *epistole* meaning *a long written message*. An Epistle is a book of the New Testament written by one of the Apostles of the early Apostolic Church and intended for instruction. The reading of an Epistle is part of the Eucharist service in the Anglican Church. The reading is selected from a portion of one of the Apostolic letters contained in the New Testament and is read prior to the Gospel reading.

Eucharist

The Holy Eucharist (or Holy Communion) is one of only two Sacraments instituted by Jesus Christ himself, the other sacrament being Baptism. The term Eucharist is from the Greek word *eucharistein*, meaning thanksgiving or always give thanks to God.

Formularies

Prescribed forms used in the service of a church. Anglican formularies are the 1662 Book of Common Prayer, including the Ordinal; the Thirty-Nine Articles of Religion; and the writings of the seven Ecumenical Councils of the Church, all of which derive from the authority of the God's Word.

Gospel

The term *Gospel* is derived from the Anglo-Saxon word *godspel* meaning *god-message*. The first four books of the New Testament books are considered to be the Gospels. They describe the life, death, and resurrection of Jesus Christ. The authors of the four gospels, in order, are Matthew, Mark, Luke, and John. The Gospel or Holy Gospel reading in the Eucharist service of the Anglican Church follows the reading of the Epistle. The Holy Gospel is read by a Deacon or Priest.

Gradual Hymn

Any hymn sung between the Scripture readings of Old Testament and New Testament.

The Great Litany

A prayer consisting of a number of supplications by a leader followed by a response by the congregation. The litany may also be performed as a chant. The litany has been known and used in the English Church since the Sixth century. The Anglican litany today is substantially similar to those used by Roman Catholics, except for the absence of invocations to the Saints or the Blessed Virgin Mary. Martin Luther hailed the Litany as one of the greatest Christian prayers ever. The fact that it is set forth as a corporate worship prayer should not deter anyone from using it personally. It is found on page 54 in the 1928 BCP, and on page 148 in the 1979 BCP.

Lent

From an Anglo-Saxon word, *lencten*, meaning spring, which is the time when the days visibly lengthen. Lent is a Christian penitential season that lasts forty days from Ash Wednesday until Holy Saturday, the day prior to Easter. It is a season of fasting and penitence (repenting of sins or offenses) in preparation for Easter.

Liturgy

A collection of formularies to be used in public worship that provides order and decorum to a church service. For example, a Eucharistic service, Morning Prayer, Evening Prayer, Noonday Prayer, and Compline are all liturgies. *Liturgy* comes from the Greek *leitourgia*, which means "the work of the people." Anglican liturgy is one in which the entire congregation participates. The central idea of an Anglican liturgy is twofold: It is Bible-based, and it consists of all God's people, both ordained and lay, actively participating with Him, and with each other, in the corporate business of worshiping

Ordinal

That portion of the Book of Common Prayer that sets forth the service and required oaths for the ordination of deacons and priests as well as the consecration of a bishop.

Ordination

The ritual used by the Anglican Church to admit a qualified individual to the Holy Order of Deacon or Priesthood. Only a Bishop may ordain a Deacon or a Priest to the Holy Orders.

Orthodox

Derived from Greek *orthos* (true or right) plus *doxa* (belief or opinion). In this instance we are talking about the Christian faith as represented in the creeds of the early Apostolic Church. Orthodox Anglicans call it the original, continuing Apostolic Faith as passed down to us by the Apostles themselves and contained in Holy Scripture, without addition or diminution (decrease).

Parish

Although the terms "parish" and "congregation" are used interchangeably in conversation, the Constitution and Canons of ACNA employ the term "congregation" only. (See "**Congregation**," above.)

Passing of the Peace

An opportunity during the church service to express Christian joy (or even to reconcile differences between members of the congregation by forgiving one another) by passing God's love to one another in the form of a greeting. Passing the peace is an ancient liturgical practice that fell into disuse until restored in the 1979 BCP, pp. 332 and 360. The celebrant says, "The peace of the Lord be always with you." The congregation responds, "And also with you." The people and clergy then greet one another in the Lord with words, handshakes, gestures, a pat on the shoulder, a kiss on the cheek, or whatever seems good and appropriate as a Godly expression of fellowship within the Body of Christ. Scriptural antecedents are Rom 16:16, "Greet one another with a holy kiss," and others such as 1 Corinthians 16:20 and 1 Peter 5:14.

Pentecost

Pentecost is the seventh Sunday after Easter Sunday. Pentecost commemorates the descent of the Holy Spirit upon the twelve Apostles and other followers of Jesus as described in the Book of Acts 2:1–31.

Presbyter

A presbyter is a member of the order of priests in churches having episcopal hierarchies that include bishops, priests (presbyters), and deacons. In the early Christian church the presbyter was an office bearer who exercised teaching, priestly, and administrative functions.

Today the title "priest" is used interchangeably with "presbyter" and is the more commonly used term.

Priest

An individual who has been ordained a priest in Christ's holy catholic Church by a Bishop. The 1979 BCP, page 531, calls the priest to "proclaim by work and deed the Gospel of Jesus Christ, and to fashion your life in accordance with its precepts. Love and serve the people caring alike for young and the old, strong and weak, rich and poor. You are to preach, to declare God's forgiveness to penitent sinners, to pronounce God's blessing, to share in the administration of Holy Baptism and in the celebration of the mysteries of Christ's Body and Blood, and to perform the other ministrations entrusted to you."

Primate

An archbishop of the Anglican Communion who is the ranking cleric of a province (national or regional church) of the Anglican Communion. (A few clerics of equivalent rank are called a "metropolitan".)

Province

The worldwide Anglican Communion is made up of 38 national or regional churches, called *provinces*. For example, The Anglican Church of Uganda (a "national church") is at one and the same time the Anglican Province of Uganda, whereas The Anglican Province of the Southern Cone is comprised of the Anglican churches in Argentina, Chile, Bolivia, Paraguay, Peru, and Uruguay, and may therefore be called a "regional church." Of course "national church" doesn't mean a national government is involved.

Rector

An ordained priest of the Anglican Church who is selected by a parish vestry (board) and approved by their bishop to serve as the administrative and spiritual head of a parish.

Sacrament

"An outward and visible sign of an inward and spiritual grace given unto us; ordained by Christ himself, as a means whereby we receive the same, and a pledge to assure us thereof" (1928 BCP, 581). The outward and visible sign of Baptism is water, while the inward and spiritual grace is dying to sin and being born as children of grace. The outward and visible sign in the Eucharist is bread and wine while the inward and spiritual grace is the Body and Blood of Christ, which are spiritually received and taken by the faithful. Only Baptism and the Eucharist are true sacraments, the only two instituted by Jesus Christ himself. Article XXV of the Articles of Religion states the matter this way: "There are two Sacraments ordained by Christ our Lord in the Gospel, that is to say, Baptism, and the Supper of the Lord. Those five commonly called Sacraments, that is to say, Confirmation, Penance, Orders, Matrimony, and Extreme Unction, are not to be counted for Sacraments of the Gospel"(1928 BCP, 607).

See

In the original sense, a *see* was the official seat (a literal chair) of a bishop, being also referred to as his *cathedra*. It was placed in the bishop's principal church. This led to calling that church his *cathedral*. *See* can also refer to the town or place where the bishop "sits," for example, the See of Canterbury. As a bishop's seat or chair was the earliest symbol his authority, the word *see* is sometimes applied to the whole area over which the bishop exercises authority, normally a diocese.

Sequence Hymn

A hymn usually sung after the reading of the New Testament and prior to the reading of the Gospel.